FOREVER AND A DAY
One last goodbye X

1 3 5 7 9 10 8 6 4 2

First published in 2013 by Ebury Press, an imprint of Ebury Publishing

A Random House Group company

The Random House Group Limited Reg. No. 954009

Addresses for companies within the Random House Group can be found at www.randomhouse.co.uk

A CIP catalogue record for this book is available from the British Library

The Random House Group Limited supports the Forest Stewardship Council® (FSC®), the leading international forest-certification organisation. Our books carrying the FSC label are printed on FSC®-certified paper. FSC is the only forest-certification scheme supported by the leading environmental organisations, including Greenpeace. Our paper procurement policy can be found at www.randomhouse.co.uk/environment

Printed and bound in Great Britain by Butler Tanner & Dennis Ltd, Frome, Somerset

ISBN 9780091957346

To buy books by your favourite authors and register for offers visit www.randomhouse.co.uk

Designed and produced by Method UK Ltd.

FOREVER AND A DAY

One last goodbye X

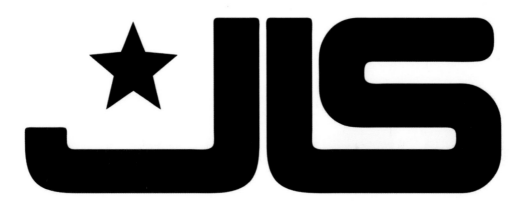

EBURY
PRESS

Introduction

We still find it hard to believe what has happened over the last six years. When we formed the band in 2007, two of us were students trying to juggle our studies with music and part-time jobs, and the other two were spending every hard-earned penny to support ourselves and chase our dreams. How did we get from there to here? From singing at family parties to going on stage in front of 80,000 screaming people, with 10 million records sold, five number one singles, five MOBO awards and two BRITs? Sometimes it's too much to take in, even now! We feel so lucky and grateful to our fans. Without you, none of it would have been possible.

Goodbyes are sad and we're all feeling the split of the band deeply. But this is also a time to celebrate our achievements and the support of our fantastic fans. We've been on the most incredible journey ever in the last few years. It's been brilliant and amazing in every way, and we have our fans to thank for that, as well as all the amazing, supportive people around us, such as our family and friends, our management and our record company. Now that we're calling time on JLS, we decided it was the perfect moment to look back over our years together and remember some of the key moments in the life of the band, from the very beginning to our final farewell celebrations. You may already know some of it, but there are also quite a few surprises, including some very personal memories.

We really hope you enjoy reading the book as much as we enjoyed putting it together. It's the ultimate JLS record of everything we have done from the very beginning to the very end, with loads of exclusive photos and our thoughts on everything from the music and tours to love, romance, our legacy and future ambitions. But the reason we wanted to do this more than anything is you. We made it for our fans, the best fans in the world, and we hope you love it as much as we do.

We love you all, JLSters!

Contents

Prologue

'To each and every JLSter, our beloved fans around the world. We wanted to make sure that you heard it from the four of us, that we have decided to bring our time as a band to an end...'

Oritsé This week we announced that JLS are splitting up, and it hurts. It doesn't matter whether it's a good or bad decision to break up, it just hurts. All my memories of putting the band together have come flooding back. I guess that's why I had a big meltdown when we were discussing the split with Alan Carr on his show, *Chatty Man*, which is filmed at the ITV studios on London's Southbank.

Before the interview, we talked to a group of fans outside the studios. All were devastated and very emotional. It was the first time we'd seen the fans properly since the announcement and it really upset me to see them upset. They were saying, 'Oritsé, why?' and asking all sorts of questions, which I did my best to answer. My heart felt heavy because we are a part of their lives; we have given them something to motivate them, we've inspired them. Some of them come from very difficult situations and I felt that the breakup of JLS was like a dream ending for them. When they broke down, I broke down with them. When they cried, I cried, even though I tried hard not to.

On our way to see Alan Carr, there was something in me saying, 'I don't want to be here right now.' Not because I didn't want to talk about it, but because I could feel the emotions welling up inside. I was unsettled before we sat down on the sofa. Walking down the stairs towards Alan is usually a really great moment because I love the show and we're friends, but this time I just felt incredibly sad. Normally I'm very talkative in interviews with him, but the words would not come – I had nothing to say.

I was fighting back my emotions all the time. 'Don't cry, Oritsé, don't get upset. Be strong,' I told myself, but I couldn't help thinking about the fans and how distressed they were because they didn't want the band to split up.

So many different thoughts were whirring round my head. I kept thinking about how I formed the band six years ago and the struggles I went through. Sometimes it's still hard to believe that I did what everybody said was impossible in single-handedly putting together the biggest UK boy band of our time. So many people tried to discourage me, but I did it on my own, through sheer determination, because I wanted to change my situation and transform my mum's life and my family's life for the better.

Now it was the end of the band that everyone said would never work. 'You are putting together an all-black boy band? You are crazy! It has never been done before in this country. You think you are the one to do it?' Then I remembered all the times I had jumped trains because I never had any money to travel. I was constantly running away from ticket inspectors. They'd catch me and push me up against the wall, gripping my arms. 'Why are you jumping over barriers?'

'I'm just trying to get to the studio, trying to do my thing,' I'd say. I tried to explain that I was working three jobs, doing my best to support my family, going to university and looking after my mum.

All this was going through my head and then I met the fans outside the ITV studios, so the most prolific moments of my life hit me at once. My head was hanging during the interview with Alan – I couldn't think about anything except how sad I felt. It was just too much. Trying to hold it all together created a big explosion and I just cried and cried. Marvin tried to comfort me. It helped to have the boys there – my brothers, my best friends.

By the end of the interview I had pulled myself together a bit, so when Alan asked us what we would like to say to the fans, I was able to say, 'Without you guys we wouldn't have had these five years of having the best times of our lives. You guys have supported us through thick and thin. You've sent us to number one five times. You've helped us win BRIT and MOBO Awards. You've made our dreams come true. For me personally, as the founding member of the band, I can't thank you enough for everything you've done for me and the boys.'

I felt we had a lot to be grateful for and people needed to be thanked. It wasn't about us having a good old time, drinking champagne with Alan; there needed to be a purpose to the interview and that was to let people know that we truly appreciate everybody who has bought into brand JLS and made four boys' dreams come true. That was important to me because people are important to me, as is showing gratitude. Right then, I felt

that it was up to me to make the point and express how we were all feeling. Somebody had to do it and I felt a lot better once I'd said it.

Marvin The day we announced that JLS were breaking up I experienced a lot of different feelings, highs and lows. We wanted it to be a celebration of our success, but I couldn't help feeling disappointment too because we were letting people down.

It really hit home when we appeared on *Chatty Man*, on a day that was full of emotion for us. Hundreds of fans had turned up to wait outside the studios and a lot of them were in tears when we went to say hello to them. 'Why? You promised you'd be together for ten years,' they said. 'Why are you doing this to us?' We weren't able to go into detail about what had led to the decision, but we did our best to reassure them that we will always be there for them in one way or another, even though the band is splitting up.

It hurt us to see their hearts being crushed by the band's split. We've always felt so much love and respect for our fans – they are the people who have put us where we are, with all their support, undying love and the precious money they have spent on tours and CDs. We're so grateful to them and we love them for everything they've done for us, so it's tough seeing them upset.

We never really imagined there being an end to JLS. When things are going as well as they did for us, you hope it's going to last forever even though you know it won't. So, making the decision to break up was very tough for us. There was a lot of confusion about whether or not it was the right thing to do, but in the end we all agreed on it. I think it was, is, and will be the right thing to do. In the last six years all of our wildest dreams have come true and it makes me happy to think of all the things we have achieved and found success with. But we never wanted to overstay our welcome – we wanted to bow out at the top.

What was against it? The fear of the unknown. We all had the same worry: 'What am I going to do? How am I going to earn money? How am I going to provide for my future or my family?' For years we have woken up and known exactly what we're doing. Everything in our lives has been scheduled, except our days off. Now, none of us knows what the future holds. That's scary after having everything mapped out for so long. It has taken me ages to get used to the idea that the day after our final show,

I will wake up and JLS will be no more. In my career, it's back to me, myself; I'll be completely alone again. What will I do?

Yet although the band is splitting up, the four of us will remain as close as ever. Without the bond that we have between us, we would never have been able to do what we've done together. Sometimes we've performed five or six gigs in a weekend, forty-five-minute sets in different venues throughout the country. You wouldn't be able to pull that off if you didn't get on and function well as a team.

Our relationship is unique: it's a brotherhood, a friendship and a business. We're a family. Our success boils down to the bond we have as four brothers. We can have a debate as business partners about a professional decision and then instantly click out of JLS band mode and be friends again. We have a massive respect for each other and we've been on an incredible journey together. In the beginning we had nothing – we were struggling to get the money together to buy studio time. We'll never forget those early days and the way we stuck together. We all believed in the magic of the band and our belief paid off.

Aston I see this as the end of an era, yet it's also the start of something new. My time in JLS has propelled me universes away from where I was before, from what I was doing and how I was living. Now it's all over and a new era is beginning. My standpoint is that nothing lasts forever – that's the best way to view endings. I am quite good at closing doors and I've seen everything in my life as an era, whether it's been athletics, football, school or my first job. I've never been that person who worries and waits for what's next.

We all have different paths in life, and right now the path of JLS is splitting into four different roads. I'm on my own now – it's just me, walking on my own path. It's no longer the four of us, side by side. Since I'm not the type of person to look back, I'm looking forward.

There has never been a moment when I've sat back and thought about everything that JLS have achieved because I've always been thinking, 'What else can we do? How can we beat that? How can we further this career and make it bigger?' I've always looked ahead to what we can achieve next.

Obviously the word 'we' has now changed into the word 'I'. So I'm now thinking, 'How can I make this bigger? How can I make my career just as successful as the last five or six years have been?' It's only one little word, but it's a huge change and very scary. Sometimes it seems like the other boys all know what they want to do in their personal and professional lives. They're 100 per cent on it, but I'm not. I'm thinking, 'Right, I've got the contacts I need, contacts that I know can help me, but what avenue do I want to go down? Is it music? Is it acting? Is it behind-the-scenes stuff, like writing?' Whatever it may be, I'm still not completely sure. It's like I'm going back to school.

For the past five years, my life has been completely structured. My diary has dictated everything I've done. Now I'm in a position where I have nothing to do tomorrow. I have nothing to do next week. Usually, there are rehearsals booked in, or singing lessons, dance lessons, gigs, photo shoots and interviews. It feels a bit funny because I'm so used to having things to do.

It would be so easy for JLS to sign another record deal and carry on. We could stay where we are and be comfortable and say, 'We're in JLS.' Whether or not we had to fight to stay at the top and go on having number ones, we would still be 'we' and 'we' is a lot easier than 'I'. But I'm not here for easy. We never entered *The X Factor* for it to be easy. We didn't join this band at a time when boy bands weren't in fashion for it to be easy. It was much more a case of, 'Believe in this. Let's do this'.

We've accomplished so much. We put our stamp on history and in the process we brought boy bands back into the equation in this country. The hysteria started with us and continued with The Wanted, One Direction, Lawson and Union J. There are quite a few boy band acts now, but we were the first boy band in ages to have a number one single with 'Beat Again' and inspire hysteria in our fans. We are proud to say, 'This is our stamp, this is what we started.' In the UK the trophy is ours, which is great. We have held our own here for all those years. There's nothing to look back on and regret.

It's an understatement to say I feel very lucky, but I've also worked incredibly hard to get to this point, as have the other three guys. They've worked the hardest I've seen anyone work. We'll always feel grateful, the luckiest four guys in the world. We're also proud of how hard we've worked for all these years and that we continued to stay as focused as we were in the beginning, when we did everything we could to keep the band going, against the odds. We did it because we believed in ourselves and our friendship – and that never changed.

For a while I had a little whisper in my ear saying, 'You know, one day you are probably going to go solo. It's going to happen.' I ignored it for ages because I was happy in the group and so it wasn't relevant. Then, when we came to the decision to bring JLS to a finish, I thought, 'You know what? I'm far from done. I can still see something happening, whether music or film, whatever. I'm still hungry.'

So, now seems like a good time to tell you that I am planning to make an album as a solo singer – and I am 100 per cent behind my new project and really excited by this new adventure. I'm writing now – I'm writing for me. It feels strange, though, because I'm so used to having the boys nearby in the studio. I'm also used to having my writing time and studio time booked into my diary, which means I can just chill when I'm not doing it. I need to get out of that mentality. It's time to see if I can turn it on without preparing myself first, if I can instantly get into the mindset when somebody calls me and says, 'I'm in the studio, what are you doing?' I'm really looking forward to it.

I'm not used to the idea yet, though. I keep forgetting that soon I won't have the backing of my three mates. It's going to be me on my own and if I want to be the best in my field, I have to prepare myself and get organised. It's a big challenge, but it's exciting. I keep thinking, 'Let me go back to square one, taste the hunger and do this.'

It's sad that JLS is coming to an end. We've been in the group a long time. It will be strange to be apart, but nothing's going to change our friendship and brotherhood, which is as strong now as it ever was. We will always have a massive bond because we have experienced things together that no one else could even imagine. Now is the time to become four individuals again and express our own individuality. It will be very interesting because it will bring out people's characters. For six years we have had to compromise. Now that we'll be making our decisions alone, where will life take us?

JB One of the main reasons I've loved being in JLS is that we have the best fans in the world. There's no arguing with that: it's a fact. I've also loved this time because of the way we are as a group. Even though some of our values may be different, we are very respectful of one another and of other people. That's so important to me and to all of us. Putting other people first is crucial, as is being kind and gentle.

At no point have any of us said, 'It's all about us.' We are the first to thank our management, our label, our families, the people around us and the people backstage – everyone you don't see, but hugely important to the whole team. For me, it all comes back to the team ethos and a shared, respectful approach to each other and the work we do.

I couldn't be in a group with somebody if they were effing and blinding all the time. It's fine to do that behind closed doors if that's what you want to do, but not in front of people. Professionalism is the bottom line. It's something we all understood from the very beginning, because of our determination to make the band work on a professional level.

I like to shine by myself but I enjoy being part of a team. For me the beauty is the way all the different pieces come together. I played a lot of rugby when I was younger and teamwork is obviously crucial to all team sports. With rugby, it's seeing all the different passes being put together to score a try. If it wasn't for the forward who won the ball in the scrum first, there would be no try. With music, it's all about the group dynamic. Everyone brings something different to the group and if you have a strong enough bond, it's amazing how powerful the unit can be.

One of the best parts of being in JLS has been travelling the world with the boys, going out in new cities, shooting videos together, hanging out with Phil from our management company and meeting industry people. Our friendship is so strong that everything has been fun and exciting. There was a harmony between us from the very start and that's something I can't really explain. The pieces of the puzzle just fitted together and our friendship quickly grew out of our shared commitment and the feeling that we had something special going on.

I've been to places that many people will never get to see, and it's all been part of my job. How amazing is that? For five years, I was lucky enough to have a very enjoyable workplace and to do different things every day. I never had any great desire for material wealth, but I was able to earn enough money to do the things that I have always wanted to do outside my work, which was mainly to travel and explore the world. I've done so many incredible things, from winning awards and accolades to travelling on a private plane.

I have no idea how I will feel when I'm by myself, without the boys. It will solely be down to me to forge my future career, which is a scary thought. As someone who enjoys doing things as part of a group, it's particularly daunting but I think if any of the boys said they weren't scared, they would be lying. Funnily enough, it wasn't until we actually made the announcement that the reality hit me. 'Wow, we really are going our separate ways!' I thought. It's hard to imagine the future. I don't think I'll properly get my head around it until our Goodbye tour comes to an end in December 2013.

In any job, people move on – they get promoted or made redundant, they have children or retire. So I see the end of JLS as moving on. Like anyone leaving a job, I don't know what the future holds. It's a life-changing decision for me, for all four of us. We are now going to be working alone rather than as a team. Whether you see it as a promotion or retirement, all I know is that I can do whatever I want to do now.

At the moment, things don't feel very different. We are still working and doing our gigs. After the summer tour, we'll have the end-of-the-year tour. We are still in the studio and we're due to go to America to do some recording for the greatest hits album, which will be released to coincide with the tour, so in many ways it feels like we're doing the same things we've been doing for the last few years. I wonder how I'll feel when it really is all over, when I look back on all the good times we shared, from getting through our first *X Factor* audition to winning our BRIT and MOBO Awards, but I'm not worried about it. I don't regret JLS splitting up, although it's a very hard thing to do.

I'm slightly disappointed that we haven't done as much internationally as I think we are capable of, especially in America. Other than that, I am very grateful, respectful and thankful for everything we have achieved, which is so much more than anybody around us was expecting us to achieve. And although the boys and I expected to do well in some shape or form, we've done so much better than we imagined we would. There have been so many milestones. We have sold a phenomenal number of records, a total of ten million units, and we've played in front of hundreds of thousands of fans. We've also won a range of different awards, from BRITs to MOBOs and Urban Music Awards. It's incredible to think that we've won five MOBO Awards, equalling the most MOBOs won by any artist or group. The MOBOs are extra special to us because they celebrate diversity in music. Winning our first ever MOBO in 2009 was a real high point in our journey and gave us such a massive boost.

For me, our achievements outweigh any personal ego or ambitions that I would have for the group, so I don't regret anything; I want to focus on celebrating JLS and what we've achieved. Having said that, it has been really tough seeing the fans getting upset about the band splitting. We have only ever wanted to make our fans happy, so it's hard. We've met a lot of our fans over the years and we've never felt anything but love for them. Our success is down to God, our fans and all the people who have supported us from day one.

Even when we're upset because of personal problems, maybe tired, or just not in the mood, every time we interact with the fans they uplift us and make it possible to go all out for them. That's why I'm looking forward to our Goodbye tour. It will be a chance for us to celebrate everything that has happened in the last six years and have a massive party with the fans.

★ ★ ★ ★

Boy Dreamers

Growing up wasn't always easy, but each of us had our dreams and found inspiration along the way. The four of us are very different people, from different areas and backgrounds, but when we met and formed the band we realised that we had all shared certain key experiences. We came from close, supportive families. We all loved music and had a talent for performing. And from an early age we were focused and determined to succeed, even if we didn't know what direction we wanted to take. There was just something inside us that drove us to work hard and do well. Here are a few special moments from our childhoods, including a couple we'd rather forget! Moments that got us to where we are today. It's time to go right back to the very start...

Aston I used to want to do everything as a kid – there was nothing I didn't want to do. Even if I couldn't do it, I'd do it. I remember one trip to Florida when I was nine, when the whole of my mum's side of the family went on holiday together. We all stayed in holiday villas on the same street. My family, my two cousins, my uncle and my auntie were all in one villa and there was a whole bunch of other relatives in the next villa along, and then the next.

We were there for two weeks and we had a brilliant time. We would go to the theme parks and I'd always put myself forward to get involved when they asked for volunteers at the shows. I never knew what I was putting myself up for, but I wanted to do it anyway, whether it was spinning plates or joining the main parade.

One day, we came across some street dancers doing amazing tricks in the middle of the park. They asked for a volunteer and I put my hand up straightaway, without knowing what they wanted me to do. 'I'll do it.'

'OK,' one of the street dancers said. 'We're going to have a dance off.'

'Cool, let's do it, let's go!' I said, and then I started trying to spin on my head and flip about.

These guys were looking on amazed, as if to say, 'Who the hell is this kid?' My mum laughs about it now.

I was a cheeky kid; I was also always the smallest kid and everyone called me 'Little Man'. I showed off all the time – it didn't matter where or when. Mostly it was Michael Jackson impersonations. Even on Christmas Day I'd put on an oversized blazer, a hat and some black trousers and start dancing in the middle of the living room for no reason other than I wanted to. 'Everybody sit down and get ready for my performance!' I'd say. I had no routine prepared – I'd just dance and make the family watch me.

Sometimes my grandparents would ask, 'Will you sing something?'

'OK, everyone sit down. I'm going to sing.' I never felt any embarrassment. Since then, I've experienced really bad nerves before big moments in the band's career, like the night we performed at the BRIT Awards for instance, but I was always fine the moment I walked out on stage.

The naughtiest thing I ever did was steal a bag of 10p Haribo sweets from the local newsagents in Peterborough. I was ten and it was one of the first times I was allowed out, just me and my friends. A group of us plotted it together. We had a great plan: 'Run in, grab the sweets and run out!'

The moment we got into the shop, we completely froze. We just stood there, doing nothing. 'Is everything OK?' the shopkeeper asked.

'Yeah, yeah.' Our faces were washed-out with fear. We were petrified. I hadn't done anything wrong yet, but I was thinking, 'I'm going to get caught, I know it.'

It felt like we were moving in slow motion. We weren't looking at what we were doing. We were watching the shopkeeper and she was watching us. Slowly our hands reached out for the sweets. 'Oh my gosh, we got the sweets!' Then we turned around and walked out of the shop as casually as we could.

As we left, the shopkeeper said, 'Bye, guys!' To this day, I'm convinced she knew.

'Bye, bye,' we said meekly.

I hate to think what my parents would have said if they had known what I'd done, which is why I didn't choose to tell them. I was brought up to be good, so I kept it to myself even though it was only a 10p bag of Haribos and I felt really guilty about it afterwards.

A couple of years later, there was a massive craze for egging houses in my area. Everyone did it – if you got bored, you bought a box of eggs and threw them at people's houses. It was ridiculous.

The local shop was always out of eggs. You'd go in and say, 'Can I have a box of eggs, please?'

'Sorry, we don't have any eggs left.'

We were twelve years old and had all the energy in the world. Sometimes we would egg someone's house and wait around to see what happened next. It would probably be a teacher or someone who lived near the school. Our adrenaline levels would be sky-high as the front door of the house opened. If it was a guy, we knew we were likely to be chased. When I look back, I think, 'Why would you do that? Why would you wait for someone to come out and chase you?' It seems like a totally insane thing to do, but back then it was all about rush.

We'd have our escape route mapped out – 'We'll cycle down the street, throw our bikes in the bushes, climb over the wall, run along the alley behind the churchyard, jump onto the roof and come down into the high street.' It was all a big game to us: we thought we were in an action film. We didn't give a thought to how annoying we must have been, or how long it took people to wash the egg off their windows.

We were so stupid in those days. One of us would stand on either side of a road, pretending to hold a length of string or wire between us. Cars would stop and people would get out and ask, 'What are you doing?'

'Nothing.' We would shrug and hold up our hands innocently.

Everything has changed so much since those days, but I still see and speak to the friends I did all those things with. It's important for me to stay in touch with my roots and where I've come from, and I often speak to people back in Peterborough. I see my family as often as I can. My mum has always been incredibly important in my life. When she became pregnant with me at the age of 19, she gave up the opportunity to go to America and train as a top chef – a massive sacrifice, which I really appreciate. She and my biological dad split up just after I was born, but then my stepdad (who I call Dad) came along when I was about three. My parents have worked damn hard to provide for the family and I've always looked up to them and admired them.

I started acting when I was eleven years old – I was in school plays and did a few bits on TV. But I wasn't sure what to do when I left school. All my friends were saying, 'I think I'm going to go to college,' but they seemed to be doing it just for the sake of it. It wasn't for me, I knew that, but what was? Should I pursue football or athletics, or follow the other side of my personality and try and make it in the entertainment industry? I decided to go to a musical theatre school and I was given a place, depending on my GCSE grades.

Then, during my GCSEs, I went for an audition for a kids' TV show for CITV called *Fun Song Factory*. My History GCSE was the day before the audition and I remember sitting in the exam room thinking, 'I don't want to do anything with History, I just want to go to my audition.'

I was offered the job at the audition. 'Great, we would like to take you,' they said. That never happens usually.

'OK, I'm leaving school now,' I decided. Getting my first proper industry job made up my mind about the direction I wanted to go in. This was it: I wanted to be an entertainer.

JB My mum brought us up to believe we could be whatever we wanted to be. She always said, 'Someone has to win, why can't it be you?'

I was born in London, but when I was very young we lived in Antigua for a while because my mum was working there. We came back to London so that my brother and I could go to primary school. At first we lived in Brixton. We didn't have much money, but I later won a scholarship to the Whitgift School in South Croydon, a great all-round private day school, and then we moved to Croydon in south London.

I come from quite a big family. My dad alone has nine brothers and sisters, so I have a lot of cousins! Dad and I share the same birthday and I remember big family parties when I was young. Relatives of all ages would be there, from babies to grandparents. When it came to my own parties, I'd want to invite the whole class. I wasn't the kind of boy who said, 'Girls aren't allowed' – I didn't want anyone to be excluded.

I'd probably say I was above the average side of naughty as a kid. There's one story my Great-Aunt J still tells to this day. She is like a grandma to my younger brother Neequaye and me and we often went to stay with her in Leicester for a couple of weeks in the summer. She grew up in Antigua and is very keen on natural remedies. There was an aloe plant growing in the front room of her two-bedroom flat and she used to put raw aloe vera in juices and make us drink them. It may be good for you, but it is disgusting, let me tell you! She also fed us vegetables all the time. Well, my brother and I hated vegetables.

On one trip, when I was about seven, we were eating our food off trays while sitting on the sofa when I hit on the idea of hiding my vegetables so that I didn't have to eat them. I couldn't put them in the bin because my aunt would have seen them, so I threw them under the sofa. It was a massive risk – if I'd been caught, I would have been in big trouble. Luckily, she didn't notice so I did it at every meal while we were there. Oh dear! When she was cleaning up after we left, she found all these rotting vegetables on the floor. I thought I'd got away with it, but she wasn't happy.

My parents were quite strict but they weren't too strict and as we grew older, they adapted. When we were teenagers, they stopped treating us like kids. Of course, there were times when I wanted to go out and I wasn't allowed. Maybe there was a school disco and I couldn't go, or I wasn't allowed out to the cinema with my mates because I

hadn't done my school homework. I probably sulked, but I never argued – I was brought up never to backchat.

When I was fifteen, I got drunk on a school trip to France and was suspended as a result. It was very unlike me to get into trouble like that – I would never have done it in England, but the older boys kept saying how easy it was to buy alcohol in France, so I went and bought some vodka. The next thing I knew, I woke up in hospital after being out cold for a while. I suppose it must have happened because I just wasn't used to drinking. Obviously I wasn't a regular drinker when I was fifteen and I don't come from a family of big drinkers.

My mum had to come out to France to collect me, which was really bad. Amazingly, she didn't say anything when she arrived. 'What? You're not even going to shout at me?' I thought. I was literally gobsmacked. She must have known there was no need for her to reprimand me because the shame I felt was punishment enough – I couldn't say a word to her. Back home, I was the talk of the school, which was really embarrassing. I had to write a letter of apology to the headmaster and to the French teacher, and I had to live with the fact that I'd made an absolute fool of myself on a school trip and everyone knew about it. It shook me up and I avoided alcohol for a while after that. It was a valuable lesson and one I have never forgotten.

Music was always a big part of my life. As well as being in the school choir and the church choir, I played the flute and the piano from an early age and joined the school orchestra for a while. I loved my music but truth be told, I didn't believe in music as a career. Classical music was all I'd been exposed to until I was in my teens and I knew I didn't want to be in a professional orchestra. I wasn't aware of all the other jobs there are in the industry; I didn't know what a musical director was. I had no idea that you could go on tour as a flutist or pianist with artists like Britney Spears or Beyoncé.

If I'd known then what I know now, there is no way that I would have stopped playing the flute and piano. But it was a school rule that if you were selected for a sports team, you had to play every Saturday – and Saturday was the day I did all my music lessons. I had to sacrifice one or the other and so I chose to continue with my sport because I couldn't see a clear path for me in music. If someone had told me about all the different possibilities, then I might have thought twice about giving up music. Everything might have been different if I'd got into acting and music earlier on in my life, like Marvin and Aston.

Still, I was very happy playing sport, although I was a little devastated when I first went to Whitgift because they didn't play football. So then I had to play rugby. My attitude was that if I had to play rugby, then I would play it to the best of my ability. Soon I developed a passion for it; I was really focused and dedicated and I went on to play for the London Irish Youth Academy and for Surrey County RFC. By my mid-teens I was playing five or six days a week and at one point considered making a career out of it.

Although the idea of being a pop star didn't occur to me, I never lost my love for music and singing. My cousin Marc worked in the music business and he encouraged me to write songs. That's when I first started thinking about music as a career. I enjoyed taking part in school concerts, plays and musicals and I formed a band in my last year at school. We performed some of my songs at a school concert in aid of charity that I organised with the head boy and a couple of other boys. It's now an annual school event, which secretly makes me feel proud.

Back in the era of Craig David and garage music, I used to sit in my bedroom writing little rhymes and raps. There were no restraints on me because I wasn't writing for a commercial market, so I was able to be very creative. I could do what I liked and the results were surprisingly good. I never saw myself as a solo artist, but I definitely started to see myself as a songwriter.

Marvin I was very focused as a boy, very determined. From a young age, I knew I wanted to be a pop star – that was it, no two ways about it. I idolised Michael Jackson and I used to watch his videos all the time. Even to this day, when I watch a Michael Jackson video it takes me back to being a ten-year-old kid again, thinking, 'Wow, what a star!' For me, he was the man: he was incredible, and I was devastated when he died.

I was brought up in a stable, loving family and that set me up for the rest of my life. My mum and dad were a mixed-race couple in the 1970s, my dad being black and my mum being white. On paper they shouldn't have made it, if I compare them to the parents of my friends at school. A lot of my friends' parents weren't together and most of my mixed-race friends' parents weren't together, so I knew I was in the minority, growing up. I also knew that my parents being together and giving me a stable upbringing made me who I am today and kept me on a steady path. That's why I'm a firm believer in family life and all the morals and values that go with it.

I was singing and dancing from the age of about four. It just came naturally to me – I loved performing! My mum and dad knew nothing about the entertainment industry, but they always encouraged me. When I was eight, I saw an ad for a theatre school in the local newspaper in south-east London. 'Do you love to sing, dance and act?' it said. 'If so, come to drama school'.

I took it to my parents and said, 'I want to do this – I want to sing, dance and act.'

There wasn't a lot of extra money as I was growing up, but they found a way to pay for me to go once a week. It was £5 a session, which was a lot of money back then. They supported me and I pushed myself; I always have done. When I was eleven I went to another drama school, D&B Performing Arts, and soon I started getting professional jobs. I played one of Fagin's gang and a workhouse boy in *Oliver!* in the West End and had small parts in *Grange Hill* and *Holby City*. But although I did bits and pieces of acting and music all through my teenage years, I worked hard at school and did well in my GCSEs too. Then I reached a crossroads and had to decide between going to college to study for A-levels or whether to pursue a career as a singer. It wasn't an easy decision at the time, but I chose singing.

When I was seventeen, I joined a band called VS, which was signed to Virgin and managed by Simon Webbe from the boy band Blue. I'd met Simon by chance at a football charity event, where I gave him a demo CD of mine on the off chance that he might listen to it. A couple of weeks later, he rang and asked if I'd be interested in joining his new band. I jumped at the chance. Three guys and two girls, we were a pop band with an R&B vibe. We went on to have two Top 10 hits, which was absolutely brilliant and I learnt so much from the experience. I'll always be grateful to Simon for giving me the opportunity to be a part of it. I was twenty when the band broke up because we lost our record deal, which dented my confidence for a while. Still, I picked myself up and got a sales job, selling land and property overseas. I did well at the job and I earned good money, but I couldn't help wondering – and hoping – whether I still had a future in music.

Oritsé When I was about four, my mum graduated from Thames University with a degree in Law. In order to study, she'd had to employ a nanny to look after my brother and me, which she found difficult. 'I'm not happy having someone else look after my children,' she told my grandmother, who also helped out.

'Well, you are going to have to make a decision,' my grandmother said. 'Either you follow your career or you sacrifice it to look after your kids full time.' It was a real dilemma for my mum, but she chose to become a full-time mother. My father works in another country, so we never saw him and my mother was more or less a single parent. I had an incredible relationship with my mum as I was growing up. She brought me up to believe that I could do anything I put my mind to. We lived at my grandmother's house in Shepherd's Bush, so she didn't have to deal with any huge financial responsibilities. My grandmother gave us a roof and put food on the table, which meant my mum was able to look after us 24/7.

We moved to a house in Fulham when I was twelve years old. Around the time of the move, my mum started passing out and collapsing. It scared me a lot because she had always been a completely healthy, beautiful and proactive mother. One day, I came home to find her in the bath, unable to move and only semi-conscious. I had to lift her out of the bath, put her in bed and call the ambulance. When she was diagnosed with MS [Multiple Sclerosis], I was distraught. Being the age I was – still only twelve - I internalised my worries. I went to school and got on with my life, unable to acknowledge how devastated I was to see my mother deteriorating in front of my eyes.

At the time I did my best to shoulder the responsibility and shield my younger brother Temi from what was happening. Also, I wanted to make sure that my mother could rely on me and know that I was there for her, whatever she needed. Suddenly the shoe was on the other foot and I had to look after her, although my grandmother was still in Shepherd's Bush and there to support us whenever we needed her. I tried to help my mum as much as I could. It was a full-time job caring for her, being there for her and making sure my brother and little sister Naomi were good too.

It was this situation that triggered my extreme determination. I became very driven, very young. While my friends were messing around and having fun, I was fully focused. I did loads of different things, but whatever I did, whether it was athletics, rugby or music, I focused on it and gave it my all. I joined the Army Cadets; I played the trumpet. Singing became a way of expressing myself and releasing my emotions. I sang whatever was playing in the house: Stevie Wonder, Bob Marley, Michael Jackson, Prince, The Jackson 5, Marvin Gaye, James Brown, The Temptations – a lot of old-school stuff. There was something in those guys' music that made me feel amazing. When I sang along, it felt like everything would be all right.

I've never had anything come naturally to me: I wasn't naturally talented at anything, I have had to work hard at everything I've put my mind to. Just as I don't naturally have a six-pack, I wasn't a natural singer. I could sing and I used to sing around the house, but being OK or good is different to being great or being exceptional. I worked hard. I've realised that I'm the kind of person things don't come easily to. That's the pattern of my life – I have to work hard to get to where I want to. The only thing that I think I'm gifted at is ideas – ideas, putting things together and having the will to do whatever it takes to make them into a reality!

Unlike Marvin and Aston, I didn't think that I was going to be a singer or an artist. I always believed that music would be my path but I didn't know how that would work out – I just knew whatever I put my mind to, I was going to do it full out. I wasn't going to do it in halves; I was going to develop and improve. All I wanted was to be successful enough to give my mum everything she needed to help her condition. I never thought it wouldn't happen because it had to happen.

★ ★ ★ ★

Magic in the Room

It all began with Oritsé and a sequence of events that led him to focus all his efforts and talents on forming a boy band instead of going for a solo career. When Oritsé brought us together in 2007, we could never have imagined what the future had in store for us. Yet each one of us knew that there was something special happening in the rehearsal rooms where we practised until late on weekday nights and over the weekends. What were we rehearsing for? Even we weren't exactly sure, although we knew we were good and believed we had a future ahead of us.

Oritsé One night when I was eighteen, I performed at a singing battle at a bar in Camden, north London. It was a live mic night and there were lots of different artists there. I went on stage wearing a trilby and sang my own song. It was cool! All I wanted was constructive criticism so that I could improve. I just wanted to know: how can I be better?

There were four judges sitting there, *X Factor* style, and they seemed to take delight in ridiculing me – they told me that I couldn't sing or write songs, I would never be a star and I had no future in the music business. They were clearly playing to the crowd, who were loving all the blind insults they were doling out; I had the whole audience laughing and heckling me. People were laughing so hard that they were falling over.

I was mature about it; I could handle it. So I stood on the stage and I listened acceptingly. My best friend Wayne was there. 'Oritsé, we should go now,' he said.

'Why?' I asked.

'Everybody is laughing at you, bro, we should go.'

'I'm not going! I want to stay until the end; they can continue to laugh at me. I want to stay until the end – I don't mind, it's fine.'

There were other performances after mine and at the end of the night a singing battle was announced. 'Have we got anybody who wants to compete?' the judges asked. I stood up straightaway. People shouted at me to sit down.

'You've already made a fool of yourself. Let's just go,' my friend said.

'No, why would I go? At the end of the day it can't get worse than it is. I have nothing to lose now.'

The referee asked my name and then said condescendingly, 'So, *Oritsé* here wants to be part of this singing battle. Will anyone go against him?'

A girl got up and the contest was underway. She sang a Mariah Carey song and everybody went crazy. 'It's over, just leave it,' people were saying to me.

I decided to sing a soulful R&B song, 'Just Friends', by Musiq Soulchild. So, I put my trilby on, got up on stage and took the microphone. Halfway through my performance, I jumped down and started serenading the judge who had given me the worst comments. I grabbed her hand and kissed it as I was singing. Everybody went wild! Suddenly the crowd was cheering for me; it was crazy. When I finished, I was announced as the winner of the battle.

'We can't believe what you've just done!' the judges said. 'Someone's just gone to get your prize.'

'I don't do music for prizes,' I said. I gave back my mic and walked out. A couple of the judges ran down the street after me, shouting, 'Call me, call me, call me! We can do something together.'

I had a lot to think about when I got home. During the evening, a girl had come up to me and shown me a newspaper article about a new vocal academy for R&B singers starting up in Dalston, the Arts Council-funded Eclipse UK Vocal Academy of Excellence. 'Why don't you try it out?' she said. 'You'll be able to develop your talent there.'

A few days later, I went down to Dalston and sang for the new academy's judging panel. I wasn't the best singer auditioning but they said, 'We feel you will go far if you are willing to work.'

'I'm willing to work harder than anybody,' I said.

They put me in the top singing class even though I was nowhere near the best. I'm not saying I wasn't a good singer but the others were exceptional, on a completely different level, technically. They came from gospel churches, whereas I just sang in my bedroom. In every way they were great singers.

There were about twenty kids in my class, which came together every Saturday for four hours. On the first day, this guy walked in and said, 'I'm going to be your singing teacher.'

'What's your name?' I asked.

'My name is Malcolm Connell and you can call me Malcolm.'

'OK, Mr Connell,' I said.

'Stop calling me Mr Connell!' he said. So I shortened it to Mr C and it stuck. After that, everybody called him Mr C.

There was something about Mr C. I really wanted to prove myself to him. At the beginning of class, he would draw a question mark on the floor, which meant that the floor was open to whoever wanted to sing. Nobody ever wanted to go first, apart from me. I always got up straightaway, stood on the question mark and started singing. Every week, I'd be the first. It got to the point where Mr C said, 'Does anybody else want to be first, apart from Oritsé?'

Then there was the way he connected with everybody. There were kids from all walks of life in the class, some of them from rough areas, with various family issues. Mr C connected with all these young people, which meant he was able to control the class and get the best out of it. I focused on trying to develop my performance skills. At the time I was doing my solo thing – writing my own songs, playing guitar and singing. At one point, I put together my own live band, with bass guitar, lead guitar, keys, saxophone and drums. Another time, I was performing on my own on the same live circuit as Amy Winehouse, Jessie J and Ed Sheeran. I had no idea about pop music; I didn't understand it. My mind was on musicianship and 'real' singing, that kind of vibe. Then again, there just weren't enough people coming to the gigs. 'Do I want to be a singer with "credibility" and no audience?' I asked myself. 'Maybe there is more.' 'I want more,' I decided.

The vocal academy closed down when its funding was withdrawn and so I approached Mr C for private lessons. I had to work hard to pay the family bills and fund my development, but determination got me through. Back then I did all kinds of jobs: I was a carer for disabled and sick kids; I touted for West End clubs and was constantly being chased away by bouncers who didn't want me selling tickets for rival clubs to their customers; I sold my CDs at university for £1, I worked for an events manager, I was a waiter and I worked as a masseur giving onsite massages in clubs. I did anything I could possibly do.

Along the way, I've met people who have really influenced me and Mr C is top of the list. He is my mentor – I look up to him and he's always there to help guide me. He always believed in me and that gave me confidence. He is a Buddhist district leader and I got into Buddhism quite heavily around this time. Mr C became like a father figure to me, especially because I don't see my dad. It happens that I was born on the same day as his son and Mr C is the same star sign as my dad. It's crazy! The relationship that we have is deep: his door is always open to me, any time of the day or night, and I spend a lot of time at his house. To this day, he gives me a lot of guidance and support.

One day, when I was having lunch with a friend at the Dance Attic Studios in Fulham, a woman came over to me and said, 'You look amazing! Do you sing?'

'Yes,' I said.

'I've got this boy band I'd like you to audition for.' She explained that she had managed Mis-Teeq for a while.

'Well, I'm doing my own thing,' I said. 'I don't really do the group thing.'

'Why don't you try it anyway?' she suggested.

I asked Mr C's advice and he said, 'Go for it.'

I went for the audition and was instantly recruited into the band, but when I met the other boys I immediately knew something wasn't right: they were trying to work out a formula and I felt that I was the token black member. We rehearsed for a couple of weeks and then they wanted to put me in a house in Hammersmith and sign me to a record label called Epic, which was under Sony on a development deal. The money they were offering would have been incredibly useful at the time, but I said, 'I really appreciate the offer and although I need the money, it doesn't feel right and I'm going to follow my heart.'

I went back to Mr C for advice. 'What do I do now?' I asked him.

'You were scouted for this boy band. Maybe this is your journey,' he said. 'Follow the patterns in your life. Maybe you are not ready to be a solo artist right now, so why not put your own boy band together? I know you can do it.' Everything led to that because I was being asked to be in boy bands left, right and centre, even though I didn't actually want to be in one.

I constructed the band in my mind and everything was set out and planned as I began to look for band members. It wasn't a case of finding a couple of boys to get together and sing with; I was looking for certain qualities and I wasn't going to accept less. Nobody was coming into the group unless they fulfilled my criteria. I looked everywhere for members – I searched online, asked around and advertised in all the music shops. I put the band together in a matter of weeks and I literally did not sleep during that time.

But I wasn't consciously intending to form a boy band made up solely of black members – I came up with a formula that I instinctively felt was right and I followed it. I was looking for people who matched and complemented one another so when I found Marvin, after meeting him through a mutual friend, I started thinking, 'Who can complement Marvin?'

I said to Marvin, 'Do you know anyone who can do backflips?' He suggested Aston. I looked Aston up on MySpace and he just seemed to fit the profile I was looking for. When I met up with him, he did a backflip and a few breaking moves. The fans love it when he does his backflips and he still does them all the time! I went home and

lined up the pictures. Aston looked great next to Marvin. Now I needed someone to complement me. Then I heard about JB through an artists' development company called Major Music, when I was scouting for my last member outside the *X Factor* 2007 auditions. Within minutes of meeting JB, I knew he was right for the band: he looked great, sang great and was the King of Harmonies.

Marvin It's hard to explain how it all started for us. From the beginning there was an amazing chemistry between the four of us; it was a really positive energy. Everything began with Oritsé. Then it was the two of us, me and him. I vividly remember meeting him for the first time at Oxford Circus, outside Niketown. As I went into the meeting, I was thinking, 'I wonder if this guy is a bit crazy. Is he talented or is he just a superfan of VS, my old band?' I didn't know.

I had given up on my music career, really – it was so tough. But the idea of being in an R&B boy band was very appealing. A few months before I met up with Oritsé, I'd seen four black guys performing at a talent competition and thought they were really cool. It was what I'd grown up on – first, The Jacksons, then from Boyz II Men to Jodeci, Jagged Edge to Damage.

After meeting him, I was sold on his concept for a boy band. I believed in him and I went for it, even though I was twenty-two at the time and thought I was quite old for a boy band. I suggested Aston might be a suitable addition to the group. He and I had crossed paths at many auditions in the past and I knew he was supertalented. I'd always thought he would be great to work with, but the right situation hadn't come along – until I met Oritsé, that is. Then we met JB.

We didn't have a record deal, a manager, money, backers or songs – we didn't have anything. But from the get-go, it was a big deal for JB to make it into the band because somehow we knew something special was happening. Although we had nothing specific to rehearse for, we had set rehearsal times, from ten to six on a Saturday, or six to ten on a Thursday night. We took it really seriously – if you turned up late, you had to pay for the whole session.

We often rehearsed in Fulham and it was probably about £40 for the day, which was a lot of money to us. One day, JB overslept and turned up about three hours late. That boy loves his sleep! I was annoyed, so I said to him, 'Well, JB, you have to pay for the whole rehearsal time.'

'OK, I'll pay it,' he said, without hesitation. I think he felt really bad that he had kept us all waiting.

We nearly called it a day after we had been together for a year. I was the only one who was earning money, through my sales job. It wasn't lots of money, but at least I was earning. Aston was in and out of jobs, left, right and centre. None of his bosses would let him have time off to audition, so the moment an audition came up, he'd leave the job. He was very ambitious and wanted to make it. For him that always came first.

JB and Oritsé were students – JB was studying Theology and Oritsé was studying Events Management – and they were broke, as most students are. It was tough for us. For a year we grafted, literally managing ourselves, styling ourselves, paying for clothes and rehearsal studios, everything. We knew we were good – we even won Best Unsigned Act at the Urban Music Awards – but it didn't lead to anything. There is only so long you can work at something without getting the results you want. In our case, the results were financial because we needed to survive: we were broke. Aston and I were living away from our family homes, so we had to support ourselves completely, which cost a lot of money, and a year is a long time when you're struggling.

Aston I first moved out of home when I was sixteen – I lived in Kent with one of the guys also doing *Fun Song Factory*. When I was seventeen, I went back home for a year and then moved out again when I was eighteen. We filmed *Fun Song Factory* for a year and then we toured it for a year. At the end of each year, I did panto, where I played Peter Pan twice. I loved doing panto, it was a really good experience. I still bump into some of the dancers I worked with in *Peter Pan* – some of them have even danced with JLS, which is funny.

In *Fun Song Factory*, I played a character called Cookie, a chef with a musical kitchen. It was great, really good fun, but at the end of two years I realised that I didn't want to get stuck in kids' TV, I had to get out. Some kids' presenters have gone on to bigger things, but I didn't want to wait around to find out if that would happen to me. I felt too young for kids' TV, I wanted to do different stuff. So I left *Fun Song Factory* when I was eighteen and started auditioning for other roles.

It was around this time that I learnt never to believe anything anyone promises until you see a printed contract with your name on it. In this industry people will promise you the world and more. If you believe them and it doesn't happen, then it's incredibly disappointing.

It happened to me while I was in *Fun Song Factory* and some of the cast was approached about forming a band. There was talk of signing with Sony and we were told there was interest from a lot of big name producers and A&R. It was music to my ears to hear all the big plans people had for us. 'I'm going to get into music, I'm going to be in a band!' I thought. I was incredibly excited. Then it just went cold; it wasn't mentioned again. That was a big blow for me.

I was back home in Peterborough, taking a break from stuff the day Oritsé called. I was playing football with some friends and the phone rang. 'I just wondered if you'd like to come down and meet me,' he said. 'I got your number from Marvin Humes – we're putting a boy band together.'

At the time, I was getting loads of similar calls from people offering this and that. I haven't got a clue why I responded to this one, but I think I started listening when Oritsé said he'd got my number from Marvin. I had only met Marvin a few times, but I instinctively trusted him. Whenever I'd seen him at auditions, I'd thought, 'This guy is cool, he's all right.' From our conversations I knew that we shared an understanding of how the industry works. So when Oritsé called, my immediate thought was, 'If Marvin is putting my name forward, it must be quite promising.'

When I went to meet Oritsé at the Dance Attic Studios in Fulham he asked me to sing first. Then he said, 'Can you dance?'

'Yeah,' I said.

I instantly liked Oritsé and dug his vibe. 'Would you like to be a part of what we're doing?' he asked me.

'Yeah, cool,' I said. 'I'll give it a chance.' All the while I was thinking that if Marv had gone for it, then it must be quite good.

Being a part of the band involved doing a lot of work for nothing, or at least without a specific goal. We weren't rehearsing for anything particular, we just wanted to be a band. There wasn't much more to it than that, other than we believed it could be good and it could be special – right place, right time, with that air of luck my mum always talks about. If it didn't work, at least we had tried.

What's funny is that I'd just put in a solo application for *The X Factor* 2007, but I scrapped that idea and joined the group because it felt like something that was working. I decided that I had to give it my biggest shot, so I moved out of my mum's back to London and into a three-bedroom flat in Camberwell with a couple of friends. There was one bathroom, a kitchen and living room, three bedrooms and the smallest garden ever. We loved the fact we had a garden, even though it was really only a square of outside space where you could fit two chairs. It was the first time I'd lived with friends and I had loads of fun.

I love my friends, but it's hard to live with a lot of people because everybody is very different. I'm the kind of person who can leave their mess for days, then I'll suddenly blitz everywhere until it's spotless. Like most people, I make a mess and clear up at my own pace, and that doesn't necessarily fit in with someone else's rhythms. When you're living together, that can cause tensions.

Meanwhile, I was struggling to pay the rent and make ends meet. I hated that phone call about the rent. 'Is your rent cheque ready?'

'Yes, it's ready.' (I just hope it doesn't bounce.)

Life was so much easier when I lived at my mum's – it was cool. But when you're older, you want to be independent; you get to a stage when you want to stand on your own two feet. 'OK, I've got my National Insurance number, I've got my provisional licence, I'm an adult per se – I don't want to have to rely on my parents anymore.'

I tried hard not to ask them for help; I'm very proud. They had to bail me out a couple of times with my rent, though. Sometimes I'd borrow against my paycheck and pay them back when I was paid, but it always left a shortfall. 'How do I get to work for the rest of the month?' I'd think. I was always racing to catch up with myself, but I never seemed to be in credit.

By the time the band decided to try for *The X Factor*, I was massively overdrawn. The bank rang and said they were going to blacklist me if I didn't pay my debt off. It was a killer – I had to go to my parents again. They said, 'We can't keep doing this.'

'I know,' I said. They started talking about me getting a steady job or going to America to start afresh. My mum said, 'There are more opportunities in America, it's bigger over there.'

I didn't know what to do. I was always broke because I kept leaving jobs when they wouldn't give me time off to do something with the band, or audition for TV and theatre work. At one point I was working in Croydon at a phone shop and sometimes I had to jump the trains to get there. I often walked from mine to the West End because I couldn't afford to get the tube. It's OK, but it gets you down not having enough money for a tube ticket.

JB I never intended to join a group. It was only after I met the others that I could imagine it working. One of the beautiful things about the group, and the reason why it has lasted a lot longer than most groups, is that we really get on with each other and have a rapport. We are more than friends: we are family. Since I'm very family oriented, it was important to me that we had that connection. Back in the day, we would go to each other's family barbecues and perform; we'd go to christenings and do little bits and pieces. Marvin DJ'd at my 21st birthday after I'd only known him for six months.

I'm privileged that I went to uni and experienced that student life as well as being in JLS. When I met Oritsé, I was in my first year at King's College, London, studying Theology. First, we met for a drink and then he asked me to come down to Dance Attic and audition. After he'd seen that I could sing – and I only sang my own songs – he asked me down again to do it again in front of Marvin and Aston. The group appealed to me because the others were prepared to work hard; they understood that I wanted to finish my first-year exams at uni before I committed to a full rehearsal schedule. And they shared my feeling for family values, respect for others and each other.

Aston When we auditioned JB, we knew instantly we had found our fourth member. All the other people we auditioned had been wrong, but he was right in every way. After he sang for us, he left the room while we made our decision. But we'd already decided. We didn't know whether it would look more professional if we left it a minute before we told him he was in the band, but then we couldn't wait and just called him straight back in to say, 'Yes, you're our final member.'

JB I believed in the group from the moment we first performed together. Early on, I said to the boys: 'We are capable of greatness. We are good enough to be taken on by someone like Simon Fuller, the Spice Girls' manager, and we are good enough to be signed by a major label like Sony.'

This was before we had written any songs, entered any competitions or even thought about trying for *The X Factor*. At the time we had been approached by Mickey Mouse managers: 'Do we want to sign a management deal with someone who is OK, who is going to give us OK songs and quibble about this, that and the other?' I asked them. 'Is there any point in going with someone who won't give us the boost we really need, or are we going to hold out for the right manager and a major record deal?'

Oritsé The best moment for me in the whole history of JLS was the moment the band first sang together. Afterwards Marvin said, 'Well done, Oritsé, you've done it! The band is complete.' I knew he was right. I felt it too, and it was the most incredible feeling ever.

★ ★ ★ ★

One Last Chance

Each of us made sacrifices to stay focused and keep the band going. But after a year of working flat out to become the best we could, there came a moment when we started to lose hope. What was the point of all our hard work, if we were heading absolutely nowhere? Was it time to stop believing? After a chance comment from JB's aunt, we decided to audition for a certain TV reality talent show and everything started to change for us, from our future opportunities to our love lives. Yaay! We discovered we really did have the X Factor...

JB Aston's mum had offered to buy him a ticket to go to America and he was thinking of going to live and work there. We were fine as a group, but we had exhausted every avenue for a year and a half. We'd entered every competition going, every best unsigned this or that, and we still hadn't been signed. We weren't being managed. What were we supposed to do? How much money can four young guys who don't come from wealthy families spend on something that is not happening? At one point we got a manager, but that didn't last long because he wanted to us to sign a contract with him, and we felt it was too early to commit.

Then we sang at a family party and my aunt said, 'You lot should definitely do *The X Factor* this year!' It wasn't anything we'd ever intended to do because we'd planned to go a different route, but by then we didn't have any other options.

'Let's go for it,' we said, a few days later. It turned out to be one of the best decisions we ever made.

Marvin I look back at *The X Factor* as the foundation of JLS. The whole *X Factor* process is like a boot camp for the music industry because you learn so much about

how everything works in such a short space of time. You are thrown into the ocean and you either sink or swim. Fortunately, we swam.

JB *The X Factor* was pure hard work. We worked twenty-four hours a day, seven days a week, literally. Everything was new to us then and we wanted more than anything to please and do well. It established a work ethic for us that we live by to this day. We rehearsed as often as we could, we did everything on time, and we were respectful to everyone. I always say that I loved being on *The X Factor* and I'd do it again if we went back in time and found ourselves back at the beginning. But if I had to do it for a second time now, no way! I wouldn't do it – it would be too much.

Marvin When we decided to enter *The X Factor*, Aston said, 'Look, boys, if this doesn't work out for us, I can't do this anymore. It's just too hard to make ends meet.' He had ambition to go over to America and do something over there – anything in the industry, really – dancing, music or acting.

That's partly why we were so nervous at the start of *The X Factor* – we knew if it was a no, it was the end of the band. We'd put in a whole year of real hard work and dedication. During that year nothing came before the band, everything was JLS. What kept us going? We believed in the four of us, we knew we had something special and we felt that something was happening in the industry. The charts were very indie and rock based at the time; there seemed to be no pop whatsoever and we felt there was going to be a change.

Aston I wasn't in a good place before *The X Factor* came along, but it was all for a reason. It definitely spurred me on during the show because I kept thinking, 'We have to do well – I can't go back to dead-end jobs and being in debt.' It made me work harder than I'd ever worked before.

On top of food and accommodation, you get paid something like £60 a week while you are doing *The X Factor*, just to cover any extra expenses you might have. It didn't really touch my phone bill, unfortunately, as I spent hours talking to my on-off girlfriend every night and my bill was something ridiculous, like £1,000, when I came out. Every

Saturday night was nerve-wracking. I couldn't even begin to think about what would happen if we didn't make it through. Then each time we made it, I'd think, 'Oh my God, the dream is still alive! We can still do this.' It was such an intense time, full of highs and lows.

Marvin Our desire to do well was something organic within the band – it grew naturally. We took our ambition seriously and worked hard to be the best we could be. Since I had experience of how a pop band should run, I was able to instill in the band how hard you have to work to make an impact. As a result, we started at such a high level of professionalism that it could only continue and get better. Everything could have fallen apart if I hadn't had that experience, as I don't think we would have taken it so seriously and given everything to JLS.

For me, that focus and determination were a product of my youth. My parents taught me that if you do something, you do it properly. You give it 100 per cent and you never do something just for the sake of it. You get out what you put in, so if you put in a little bit, you are going to get out a little bit; you put in everything, you are going to get everything in return.

I learnt a lot from my job in sales about positive thinking. There was a particular quote from Henry Ford that kept coming back to me. 'Whether you think you can, or you think you can't – you're right'.

The fact is that if we wanted JLS to work, it would work. If you want something to happen, you can make it happen. If there was any doubt or negativity – if we weren't giving enough to the band – that would be the reason why it didn't work. Knowing this, we made sure there was no margin for error, no room for being slack. Then, if it didn't work, we would know that we had done everything we could have possibly done.

Back then, when you auditioned for *The X Factor* you signed a contract agreeing to sign with Sony and be managed by Modest! Management if you got to a certain stage in the competition. That was fine with us. We would have signed anything because we just wanted to make it. After we signed, we made it through the Judges' Houses stage and into the live finals, which was incredibly exciting. We were on our way to making it!

Two days before we moved into the *X Factor* house, I had a phone call from one of the programme's lawyers. She called me rather than one of the others because I was the unofficial spokesperson for the band, I suppose. 'Marvin, I don't know how to tell you this but it's looking like you and the boys are going to be disqualified from the competition,' she said, sounding really downhearted.

My world came crashing down as I heard her words. I started panicking. 'What the hell? What's happened? Has someone done something wrong?' I thought.

She explained that there was a problem because of a clause in a contract we had signed a year before, when we had entered another competition for unsigned acts. The competition prize was to be managed by Beyoncé's dad, or something like that, but we didn't win and soon forgot all about it.

The problem clause in the contract we had signed stated that if you were offered a record contract within two years of signing the contract, then the company issuing the contract could match your record deal and get first rights over you as an act. It meant that if Sony offered us a deal off the back of *The X Factor*, this other company would have had priority over them. For Sony, that would have been completely unacceptable.

'But we know the guy we signed the contract with,' I told the lawyer. 'He is a positive guy. Why would he want to hold us back?'

'We can't take the risk,' she said. 'If you win the show and somebody else signs you, Sony are screwed.'

'Are you saying we might be thrown out of the competition?' I asked. 'Leave it with us,' she said. 'We'll talk to this guy and see what he's saying.'

My first thought was, 'Oh no, I can't tell the boys this!' I didn't want any negativity around us – we were so excited to think that this could be our time. We were the only boy band on the show. There were two girl bands in the Groups category, but no other boy bands so I couldn't tell them that we were about to be disqualified.

I had a totally sleepless night over it. I tried to call the guy we had signed the original contract with but he wouldn't take my calls. 'Surely you are not going to hold us back?'

I thought. 'Surely you are proud of what we have achieved?' But since he wouldn't pick up the phone, I had to assume that he wasn't going to let us go.

The next day, the lawyer rang to say that he had released us. I was so relieved – it was the best phone call ever! It meant that I didn't have to tell the boys anything. I did tell them afterwards, but not for quite a while and certainly not until after the show was over. That came down to experience for me because I just didn't think the boys needed to know and I didn't think it would do any good to tell them.

JB I met my girlfriend on the show. She wasn't really saying very much when we had our first conversation – she just stared at me. I always joke with her that she was in awe, but she says she wasn't. It was just that it was her first job and she was nervous.

'Hi, I'm JB, what's your name?' I said.

'Chloe,' she said shyly.

I had already met a dancer called Chloe, so I said, 'OK, you are Chloe T and she is Chloe S. Nice to meet you.'

There were only six dancers on the show that week, whereas in previous weeks there had been as many as fifteen. So, even though she wasn't dancing with us, we got to know each other a bit as the week went on because there was a lot of hanging around during rehearsals. We exchanged numbers at the end of the week and kept in touch, messaging and stuff.

She and the other Chloe came to see us in the *X Factor* house in Hampstead, north London, when they were in the area. On Sundays, me and the boys had as much free time as we ever got, which was an hour, when we'd head off to the pub down the road from where we were staying. Chloe joined us a couple of times, but we didn't have any scheduled dates.

Then, one Thursday night, we agreed to meet without everyone else there. Looking back, I suppose it could be classed as our first date. We set the time at 8–8.30 p.m., after I'd finished filming for that week's *X Factor* videotapes (VTs) 'We should have time

to get some food and chill, and go to the cinema,' I said. (The curfew for getting back to the house was around 11 p.m.)

We started filming our VTs at 6.30 p.m. Usually we completed them quite quickly, within an hour and a half maximum, but for some reason it took four hours this time. Meanwhile, Chloe arrived at the pub down the road at 8 p.m. Since I didn't know how much longer I would be, I messaged her and said, 'Just hold on. Go and get a seat and as soon as I'm done, I will be over.'

An hour went past. I kept messaging her during all the little breaks we had – 'It's taking so long, sorry.' Another hour went past. 'I'm so sorry!' I messaged. What could I do? I kept her waiting for two and a half hours and when I finally got away, I had ten minutes before the curfew.

Oritsé I fell in love with Aimee Jade – AJ, as everyone calls her – the first time I ever saw her. I really did. She was working on *The X Factor* when we were contestants. Lots of the dancers used to hang around us, trying to get to us, but AJ would come in and do her job, do it to the best of her ability and leave, which was very different.

The first time I noticed AJ, I was transfixed. When she walked into the room, there was just something about her – it was more than her beauty. There was something else about her that mesmerised me. At the time I was dating Ruth Lorenzo, another of the *X Factor* contestants, so it was a strange situation. Ruth saw me looking at AJ. She tapped me and said, 'Stop it.'

A beautiful and talented solo singer, Ruth was five years older than me and she had a lot more experience of life. We were drawn to each other during the early stages of *The X Factor* when the contestants came together in London after the first round of auditions. Then I found out she was in a relationship, so I stepped away.

At the first stage of boot camp, Ruth started telling me that she was no longer with her partner. 'I want you, but I can't have you,' she said.

She began to get jealous when I looked at other girls in the competition. I said, 'Ruth I can't be with you.'

'But I still feel you are cheating on me by looking at other girls,' she said.

'How can I be I cheating on you when we are not even together?' I asked. It was confusing. She had so much more life experience than I did – she was in a relationship and owned a house, whereas I was a really late bloomer.

When everybody came back from boot camp, we stayed at the Novotel in Greenwich. That's where Ruth and I shared our first kiss. I went to her room, she gave me a massage and we ended up kissing. Nothing else happened until we went into the *X Factor* house together, when it went to a different level, intense and passionate. One night she texted me to say, 'Are you awake? Come and see me.'

'Where are you?' I asked.

'In the bath,' she replied.

I sneaked out of the room I was sharing with the boys and crept upstairs (the girls were upstairs and the boys were downstairs). I went very quietly because you weren't allowed to leave your room after curfew time, let alone mingle with the girls. There were housekeeper/researchers who were supposed to be keeping an eye on us, so I had to be very careful.

I got into the bath with Ruth and that was the first time we had an intimate moment. After that, I was completely distracted by my passion for her. We were constantly having secret trysts in the house undercover; it was really exciting. Things between us were fiery. Almost every night I'd sneak up to her room after everybody went to sleep; it was crazy. I had to make sure I didn't disturb Alexandra Burke, who was also sleeping in the room.

I was completely into Ruth and I felt she was completely into me. We did our best to hide what was going on and I think we succeeded. People could sense there was something between us, but they had no idea what we were doing after dark. I'd sleep in Ruth's bed and then she'd wake me up around 4 a.m. so that I could creep back to my room without anyone noticing. In the morning I'd be so tired that I often fell asleep sitting on the side of my bed because I'd been up all night with Ruth. Obviously the boys knew what was happening but they didn't say anything. They knew there was this Spanish fire blazing – I couldn't fight it.

While all this was going on, I saw AJ for the first time. Lightning struck and I was completely besotted with her from afar. 'Wow, this girl!' I thought. She was so beautiful and natural; I instantly felt drawn to her. For weeks I didn't have the courage to say anything to her, but one day she caught me sneaking a look at her through a door when she was with the other dancers.

By now I was realising that I was in an impossible situation with Ruth, but I couldn't get out of it – I was too caught up in the passion of it all. I was so new to relationships that I didn't know what all my feelings meant, or how to interpret her behaviour. I was still fairly innocent and what happened between us had taken me by surprise. Up until that point, all I was concerned about was music, family and surviving, that was it. I thought about girls but they weren't my main preoccupation. My focus was my career, my ambition and my mum.

I was very cut up the day Ruth was voted off the show in Week 8. It was then that I realised how much my feelings had grown for her. Her partner was still around and everyone was warning me to stay away – 'Oritsé, she has not broken up with him. They are still together'. But I was young and susceptible. They did break up and I stayed with her for about six months after that.

Everybody but me knew that Ruth just wasn't right for me. I was totally caught up with her because she was magnetic, attractive and so much more experienced than I was. Back then I didn't understand myself too well. I was quite unsure of myself and I wasn't body confident. I would be constantly covering up because I didn't feel 100 per cent, so I wasn't prepared for love or fame or anything – I really was still feeling my way in life.

Aston A few weeks before the *X Factor* final, we found ourselves in the bottom two, in danger of being voted out of the competition. It was a massive scare, but we managed to come back from it by working even harder and staying focused. Then, a week before the final, we went to Croydon, JB's hometown, for our '*X Factor* homecoming'. That's when we saw the madness that was starting to surround JLS – it was crazy. Just being there, our presence, caused almost total shutdown in Croydon.

'How the hell has this happened? What have we done?' I wondered.

Our destination was Fairfield Halls, but we couldn't get near the place: we were in our car for hours while more police and ambulance staff were drafted in to deal with the mayhem. They couldn't let us out because the crowds of people were going mad. Everywhere, young girls were trying to knock down the barriers, stampeding to get into the building. 'Boys, you'll have to stay in the car,' we were told. 'It's full inside the theatre and there are thousands of people outside trying to get in.'

We couldn't believe it – we were just four guys from a TV show. When we finally got out of the car, the noise exploded. There's a photo of us showing a look of sheer amazement on our faces – 'Oh my God!' It was a scramble to get inside the building. There were arms coming at us from every angle. Inside was a massive room, just full of police. 'We are sorry, really sorry,' we told them, even though we didn't know what we were apologising for. We didn't know what we had done.

That night, I kept thinking, 'We are going to do this. We are really going to win this.'

Another day, we went back to my old school. There were hordes of people outside. I could see all of my friends, people I didn't know and even people I didn't like. 'This is crazy!' I thought.

When we came second to Alexandra Burke, I was so upset and annoyed. I thought, 'Oh no, this is it, the end!' We thought it meant that we would have to go back to rehearsing again. 'How am I going to live? What am I going to do?' I wondered. I had moved out of my flat just before we went onto the show and I was staying with my girlfriend. Was I about to end up back at my mum's with no money and nothing to show for myself?

The first clue I had that my life had totally changed was when I went home for Christmas after *The X Factor* finished. Me and my dad took a walk to Sainsbury's to get a few things. We were walking down the fizzy drinks aisle behind two little girls and their mum when one of the little girls turned around. She saw me and froze. I didn't think much about it because I'd been in the *X Factor* bubble. The crowds in Croydon had been amazing, but I thought that hysteria would all go away now the show had ended and we hadn't won.

'You all right?' my dad asked the little girl.

Suddenly she started screaming and crying. An onlooker would have thought my dad had hit her or pushed her over, or something.

'What's wrong with her?' I thought. 'She's having some kind of breakdown.'

Her mother told her to calm down. 'No,' the girl cried out. 'It's *Aston*!'

I didn't know how to deal with it. 'What do I do? Do I walk away? Do I give her a hug?'

In the end, I gave her a hug and she collapsed on me. 'You don't realise the effect you're having on people, do you?' my dad said.

'I think I'm starting to get an idea,' I replied. 'Wow!'

★ ★ ★ ★

Whirlwind

When The X Factor came to an end, we went through a time of uncertainty. We were working and earning money – and people seemed to love us wherever we went – but we didn't have a record deal, so it felt like we still weren't going anywhere. When our management came through for us and we signed to Epic Records, the buzz around JLS grew. We started work on our first album and recorded our first two singles, 'Beat Again' and 'Everybody In Love' and both of them went to number one. Then our album 'JLS' went straight to the top of the charts. Suddenly we were in the fast lane, performing in front of massive audiences, taking planes to LA, shooting videos and winning awards. It was the beginning of the JLS whirlwind, when every day held a new and brilliant experience. We just couldn't believe it was happening to us!

JB When we came out of the *X Factor* house at the end of 2008, I went home, washed some clothes, packed my bags and then left home for three months. The boys and I went all over the place. First, we did the ChildLine gig in Dublin and then we did gigs up and down the country over Christmas and New Year, including on New Year's Eve. We said to our management: 'We want to be working. We'll do three gigs a night, every night, if necessary.' They took us at our word and we've never worked so hard in our lives.

We literally travelled the length and breadth of the country, performing and promoting ourselves. We'd go from Sheffield to Hull to Grimsby, to Mansfield to Manchester to Birmingham and to Stoke within forty-eight hours. Every night, we'd be on stage at the first club at 9 p.m., at the second club at 11 p.m. and at the third club at 1 a.m. We usually sang four songs, including a couple of acapellas, before heading off into the night to the next venue. Thousands of people saw us perform and I think that's part of the reason why the first singles and the album did so well, because our fans felt a personal connection with us.

These days, all the *X Factor* acts do a similar club circuit when they leave the competition, but back in 2009, we instigated it because we wanted to keep working and build on our success. After two months of doing our own gigs, we went on the *X Factor Live* Tour and supported Lemar on The Reason Tour, which was brilliant because he was fantastic to us and we learnt a lot from him. Those were really exciting times. I loved going out on stage at the O2 Arena in front of 15,000 people during the *X Factor Live* Tour – the atmosphere was amazing and I couldn't stop smiling. When we came off, I said to the boys, 'Next time we go on that stage, I want us to be the headline act.'

I was speaking to Chloe all through this time but I was hardly home, so you couldn't have said we were dating. We just didn't have enough time together and the band got busier every day. We toured, we wrote and recorded our first album, *JLS* and we went hard on the promo trail. We had a sense that 'Beat Again' [our first single] would do well after it had been delivered to radio because the DJs started playing it straightaway and everyone seemed to love it. But we had no idea what the future held and we wanted to give ourselves the best possible chance to succeed.

Oritsé Ruth rented a flat and I moved in with her after *The X Factor* finished. Then we went off on the *X Factor Live* Tour together. Once we were back, it got kind of complicated and things soon went downhill. One night I came home to find her in a candlelit situation with a dancer from the *X Factor* tour. He was trying to get with her even though he knew I was with her. We had a two-week break after that. I went back to my old neighbourhood and stayed at a neighbour's house because at the time I had no money. Then, while I was on tour doing club gigs with the band, I spent the night with a fan, which was a silly thing to do because even though Ruth and I weren't officially together at the time, I think I did it because I was feeling hurt and confused. I was out of my depth and I thought it would help me feel better about myself, but of course it didn't, instead it just caused more hurt and confusion.

Ruth and I met up afterwards and decided to get back together. She had a fit when she saw scratches on my back, which were still there after my night with the other girl. She said I'd cheated on her, even though we weren't together when it happened. We had agreed to have a break, but we were still together as far as she was concerned. It was a mad situation and none of it made sense to me. We weren't right for each other, clearly – that's the truth of it. Everybody could see it, apart from me. Finally, it ended between us. She came back from another series of gigs and when I opened the door to her, I could see in her eyes that something had changed. I don't know what had happened, but it was the final straw: it was over.

Aston I went back to my mum's for a day and then we went to Ireland to play the O2 Arena in Dublin at the ChildLine gig, alongside Westlife, The Script and The Saturdays, among others. That was amazing, a taste of what was to come. We still didn't know that things were going to happen for us, though, because we didn't have a record deal. Everything else was totally cool. We had new management, we were doing gigs up and down the country and money seemed to be coming out of nowhere. It was like, 'What is this? It's absolutely ridiculous. We go out to these clubs and sing these songs, and everybody is going absolutely nuts for us'. Of course, we loved it.

It began to feel like the band was really kicking off. We thought, 'Cool, all is good, but we don't have a record deal.' Still, the money was coming in, so we couldn't complain too much. It was boom, boom, boom! And it wasn't long before I had a call from my bank, saying, 'There seem to be a lot of irregular amounts coming into your account and some of them are quite large sums. Is everything all right?' It was an awkward phone call. 'What do I say?' I thought. 'Do I try and explain the situation or just say I've started a new job with strange amounts of money coming in?' I knew either explanation would probably sound weird.

'It's all good, it's fine,' I said. 'I've just started a new job.'

'OK, well good luck with that.' From there it was just a case of: 'Right, let's go for this, boys! Let's really go for it.'

Marvin and I found a flat in north London and moved in together. I think the biggest thing for me around that time was being able to pay a year's rent in advance. Everything else was great, but that was the best of all. It was such a relief! Our advance wasn't much and we had to share it between the four of us, but we had money coming in from doing three gigs a night, every night and then we did the *X Factor Live* Tour and were paid for that. I remember thinking, 'This is ridiculous! My account used to say minus £600 and now there's no minus, just zeros. What the hell is going on?' It was great being able to pay my parents back and treat my sister and brothers to some new clothes.

It was weird going from one extreme to the other, and it was long before we'd made our album. We didn't even have a record deal, but I had a nice black 207 sport Peugeot and lived in a great flat, with a new TV and everything. I didn't lose my focus, though, because I knew there was so much I wanted to achieve.

Oritsé It was all well and good having management, but we weren't going anywhere without a record deal. There was a real buzz about JLS, so we couldn't understand why it wasn't happening. I wondered if it was all over for us. Since we hadn't won *The X Factor*, would we now disappear into obscurity? It could easily happen. If things did go that way, I decided, maybe I would become a postman. I wasn't going to give up on music, but working as a postman would keep me fit and financially afloat. The other advantage was that I could do early shifts and have the rest of the day and night to pursue music.

Our management company kept saying, 'Don't worry, just be patient – it will happen.' But we had been waiting for stuff to happen ever since the band first got together and now we were getting agitated; we desperately needed a deal. Eventually they sat us down and dropped the news that we were going to be signed by Epic Records. Unbeknown to me it was the same label that had offered me a deal in the band they were developing when I was scouted in Dance Attic and that same band never worked out. Being signed to Epic was the best news ever! We were so relieved.

Marvin Now it was time to work on our first album. 'Everybody In Love' was one of the first tracks to be sent to us and we loved it immediately. It was originally

called 'Forever And A Day' because of the line 'I'd wait forever and a day for you'. But we changed it because we felt that 'Everybody in Love' was a title that reached out to every one of our fans and listeners. It gave us goosebumps when we heard it and it just seemed to sum up the spirit of JLS. It's the reason we've called our last book *Forever and a Day* because that song meant so much to us and now those words have even more meaning. We were all agreed that it should be our first single, but the record company had other ideas. We didn't know then what we know now, which is that Nick Raphael and Jo Charrington at Epic totally understood the JLS vibe and had a great sense of how to shape the beginning of our career.

'Beat Again' was one of the last songs to come through. I wasn't sure about it at first and Oritsé and Aston shared my doubts but we felt differently after we had made some changes to the structure and gone into the studio to record it. It sounded great. A week after we recorded it, Radio 1 played it for the first time on 8 May 2009. We went mad when we heard it. We were in the studio with Steve Mac, who co-wrote it with Wayne Hector, and he put it through the studio speakers when it came on. Wow! It was an incredible moment.

JB We spent May and June working intensively in the studio on the *JLS* album. It was the calm before the storm, although we didn't know it at the time. Things blew up for us in July 2009, when we had our first number one single and everything went crazy. Nobody expected it. Neither our management nor our label thought we would have a number one single, let alone two number one singles in six months. We were the runners-up on *The X Factor*, we'd come second – no one thought we'd be winners after that. After 'Beat Again', you could see that the second single and the album were going to be huge, but not before then.

Aston I believe there's a reason why we didn't win *The X Factor*. There is a reason why we didn't sign to Syco [Entertainment, Simon Cowell's company] and went with Epic instead. There is a reason why 'Beat Again' was our first single and not 'Everybody In Love'. If it's meant to be, it's meant to be and it will happen. You just have to go along with it.

I think it made a difference that we didn't release 'Everybody In Love' first. It was definitely the right decision and we owe it to Epic A&Rs Nick Raphael and Jo Charrington.

There are not enough people like Nick and Jo in this industry. They care as much about what happens to their artists as the artists do, and that's rare. While we were working with them, they invested as much in their craft as artists do and their craft was finding good songs and creating good strategies for new acts. For them, it wasn't about getting a bonus or making money for the company: they did what they did because they wanted the best for us.

Although my instinct told me that 'Everybody In Love' should be our first single, I trusted Nick and Jo's business savvy and the fact they had our interests at heart. Then we got our first number one with 'Beat Again' in July, which made me trust them even more.

I knew how much I wanted it to go to number one and how happy I would be if it did. I didn't know what would happen if it didn't, but since we didn't win *The X Factor*, I wasn't expecting 'Beat Again' to go to number one. In some ways I didn't understand how it did get to number one, but your faith grows when something like that happens – you want to scream and shout about it. After that we had a massive party and it was amazing; it was crazy! Those days were the best – dangerous days, happy days.

Marvin My wonderful nan died in the week that 'Beat Again' went to number one, so I experienced the lowest low and the highest high within the space of a few days. On the day we were officially confirmed at number one – 19 July 2009 - we played T4 on the Beach at Weston-super-Mare. The atmosphere was amazing; it really was a wicked vibe. That evening, we had a party to celebrate at Aston's and my flat. Each of us invited twenty people and it was one of the best evenings of my life.

JB After 'Beat Again' went to number one, everything was a bit of a whirlwind for me, to be honest. I don't remember any of it in any great depth. It was a massive learning curve because every day I was doing something new, things I'd never expected to be doing. It was a very enjoyable time. I loved it, especially going over to LA, where we filmed the video for the second single, 'Everybody In Love', and spent a couple of weeks in an LA studio, writing for the *JLS* album.

The 'Everybody In Love' video shoot was in huge contrast to the 'Beat Again' shoot, which was a performance video, filmed in a studio. 'Everybody In Love' was more sophisticated, I suppose you could say – it had vignettes and a storyline. For me, the song underlined what JLS were about and it's my favourite JLS song to this day. What I love about it is that the lyrics are universal and inclusive of everybody. The song is not just about romantic love, or directed at one person: it addresses everyone.

It was brilliant to go clubbing in Hollywood and shopping in Rodeo Drive while we were in LA. It wasn't the travelling that was new to me because I had been to Japan before I'd left school. I'd been on a plane and I'd travelled in business class. Those things were brilliant, but they weren't a novelty. What was new and exciting was being there with the boys, meeting people from the record company, going out to the famous LA diners, everything. The camaraderie was the most important part of it for me, along with visiting the labels and learning about the music industry.

Oritsé Back in London, the boys were telling me that they kept bumping into my *X Factor* crush, AJ, while they were out. 'She's amazing!' they said, knowing how much I liked her. They knew the Ruth situation, so I guess they were gently trying to encourage me to move away.

There was something about AJ. It was partly her energy, and she was incredibly hot. One night after Ruth and I had split, I was in a club and I saw a girl band performing. Their music was R&B pop and everybody was going crazy for them – they had so much personality and individuality. 'Who is this band?' I wondered. Then I saw it was AJ.

Afterwards, I went up to her and said, 'Your band is amazing! I would love us to work together somehow.'

Originally from Manchester, AJ was not only the founding member of the band, but also its manager at the time. Like me, she had put together a band – only hers was a girl band. She agreed that I would take on a mentoring role and together we worked to find Vida a good management company. We were really going for it, trying for the big break.

AJ and I found we had a lot in common; we understood each other. It was a very natural feeling and it caught me in a very positive way. There were so many points of comparison – I put JLS together, she put Vida together. She had a similar driving ambition to me. We worked well together and soon became friends.

Just before 'Beat Again' came out in July 2009, I remember calling her and saying, 'Check our first video out! Call me back when you've seen it.' I was trying to impress but she didn't call back.

'Why didn't this girl call me back?' I thought. I lifted up my phone – 'Shall I call her?' I knew why she wasn't impressed. In the end I called her: 'Did you see the video?'

'Yes,' she said.

'What did you think of it? You didn't like it, did you?' I asked.

'No,' she said. She was that honest with me from the beginning. Then she told me all the reasons why she didn't like it – 'You need to take your performance to another level, your swagger and how you are. Everything. What you're doing on the video is not good enough.' That's when she started to help me as a performer. She gave me ideas all the time.

I don't really like watching the 'Beat Again' video because I agree with her 100 per cent. I'm proud of it but I wasn't the performer I am now. I was very erratic – I just wanted to be jumping about doing everything. It's so different now and when Oritsé is on stage, people are drawn in, but for the right reasons. It's not because I jump about everywhere but because I'm in the performance; I'm contained and I know how to express myself through movement and through singing. My performance is much more natural now – it's cool.

Marvin We recorded the 'Everybody In Love' video in LA in early August 2009. It featured four beautiful actresses and a cast of extras and was a big step up from the 'Beat Again' video. I think that's because nobody was sure how successful we would be, so it would have been too much of a risk to spend big money on our first video. That's the business side of it, really – it's probably the same for a lot of people who come off *The X Factor*.

Watching 'Beat Again' does make me cringe a little now because it's so long ago and we have developed so much since then, both in our dance moves and our general presence on screen. Don't get me wrong, I don't look at it and think, 'I hate that!' I don't feel that

way at all because it is part of our history and always will be – I will never forget that. But if you asked me what my favourite video is, it wouldn't be 'Beat Again'.

JB Our dancing has definitely improved. You can ask Chloe. She hates the 'Beat Again' video because it just looks terrible and nobody is on time, so she says. I defend it by saying that we only had two days to make it. It was during that time when we were manic, doing gigs up and down the country and trying to fit everything into the spare minutes we had. These days only having two days to shoot a video isn't a problem because we have so much muscle memory. We have to dance all the time and turn things around so swiftly that we pick up moves and routines far more quickly.

Marvin At the end of August, we found out that we had been nominated for two MOBO Awards. We could not believe it, especially as we had only released one single so far. A month later, we flew up to Glasgow for the MOBOs full of wonder and excitement. The nominations were for Best Newcomer and Best Song for 'Beat Again'.

In the Best Newcomer category, we were up against Alexandra Burke, who had famously beaten us in *The X Factor* just under a year before. We were desperate not to come second to her again, so it was amazing when it was announced that we had won. We couldn't stop hugging each other and jumping up and down. Then we went on to win Best Song, even though we were up against Tinchy Stryder, N-Dubz and Dizzee Rascal. We were genuinely shocked, and very, very happy.

As you can imagine, we partied hard that night. To top everything, we met La Toya Jackson, Michael Jackson's sister, at the afterparty. It's rare to see Aston lost for words, but when he was introduced to La Toya, he was absolutely speechless!

2009 just kept getting better and better – and busier and busier. Our debut single went to number one, our second single went to number one and then our debut album went to number one on 17 November, my mum's birthday, outselling Robbie Williams's album *Reality Killed The Video Star* by 2,000 units. Nobody dreamed we'd have that kind of success, so it was amazing – we were over the moon!

Oritsé My favourite video is 'One Shot', the reason being that we got to work with a legendary choreographer. It was actually AJ who told me about him when we were first talking, back in the day. 'You guys should work with a guy called Marty Kudelka,' she said. 'He's choreographed for people like Justin Timberlake. He'd be really good for you.'

We filmed 'One Shot' in late November and it was definitely one of our best-choreographed videos. I felt we looked international in it. The slickness was also down to the video directors, a duo called Rich + Tone Talauega. They came from a choreography background and they'd worked with people like Michael Jackson and Chris Brown. 'One Shot' was their first video and they put everything into it, even though we made it on a really small budget.

I just loved everything about that video. It had a really streamlined look and I loved our outfits. We looked great and felt great. From a creative perspective, we looked the best we have ever looked. When I watched it back, I thought, 'We are good!' It was a basic, classic performance that gave us an iconic look, especially the last shot of our silhouettes, each holding mirrored positions. I felt everything about the video was wow!

I'm sure that 'One Shot' would have been number one had it come out before the album. It still did really well and was great for us. Sometimes it's not so important to concentrate on chart positions. I like what a song does for your career and I felt that 'One Shot' introduced us to a wider audience and recruited new fans across the board.

JB 'One Shot' is kind of a romantic song, as well as being quite aspirational. It was a brilliant single, the third single off the album, and I agree with Oritsé that it probably would have been a number one, had it been released before the album. I really enjoyed making the video – it's definitely one of my favourites, along with 'Eyes Wide Shut'. The directors were brothers who have worked with some of the biggest artists in the world and they took us up a step with the choreography, imagery and everything. It had a powerful impact and we all looked great.

Oritsé My career took off and I was everywhere, but AJ and I stayed close and our friendship grew stronger. We'd be on the phone for hours and hours. I found her very genuine, patient and heartfelt. She didn't want to know me because of my fame, or anything like that. When there were paparazzi waiting outside clubs or restaurants we went to, she would walk around them to avoid them. We were best friends for a long time before anything romantic happened and that's the way we both wanted it. Having a girlfriend wasn't a priority for me because I was so involved with my career – and she was very focused on her band.

JB Chloe and I didn't really have any kind of formal relationship until the end of 2009. By then we had been seeing each other for long enough that we both wanted to know what the situation was: were we going out? I guess we felt like a couple, so we decided to make it official.

Chloe jokingly complains that we don't have an anniversary for when we first got together, and it's true. Life was so turbulent around then – we didn't know where we were. For almost a year after *The X Factor*, there wasn't much time for family, girlfriends or any kind of private life. It was difficult.

Life didn't exactly slow down for JLS after the first year, but we had a chance to pause and take stock. We released the first album, *JLS*, in November 2009 and its success gave us the impetus to book our first headline tour. Although we were busier than ever, we had done the bulk of the hard graft needed to establish ourselves. All the really time-consuming work was behind us, for a while. We didn't need to be out there touring the clubs and visiting every local radio station as we looked ahead to writing our second album and geared up to our tour.

At last I could spend a bit more time at home, which meant I could see more of Chloe, who lived about fifteen minutes away in Epsom. I was still based at my family home then. Chloe and I often went into town together, to clubs, restaurants and shows, but we also did a lot of stuff locally because I'm very much a local person. Even now, one of my favourite places to go is the local pub, which is five or ten minutes down the road from my house.

Aston I'm really glad that I enjoyed the first stage of JLS so much. There I was, aged twenty-one, living with Marvin in an amazing flat, driving an amazing car, being able to go away for work and just being so appreciative of everything. It was all unbelievable and amazing – it was rainbows and sunshine and I enjoyed every minute of it! For a while, I lost my hunger and ambition because I had everything I could have dreamt of; I was satisfied. I just went along with the ride and I loved it.

Later on, all of that breaks down a little bit. You start learning about the nitty-gritty side of music, you become savvy to the charts and how the industry is working, and you see how labels work with their release schedules and artists. I'm so much more aware of everything than I was back then, when everything was new and I was too excited to analyse anything. I remember thinking, 'Wow, this is amazing! I'm in a band and it's getting bigger and bigger. I can't believe my life – I love my life.'

Top of the World

Our debut album hit the one million mark and just kept on selling. We travelled around the country on a sold-out theatre tour in early 2010 and then we won two BRIT Awards – one of the most amazing nights of all of our lives. Marvin began dating his future wife and before long we were back in LA, writing and recording tracks for our second album, 'Outta This World'. We were crazy busy and loving every minute of it. Our first single from 'Outta This World' went straight in at number one and towards the end of the year, we were asked to release the BBC Children in Need single 'Love You More'. It was a massive honour and privilege to be able to use our position to make a difference to people's lives. Something we'll never forget.

Aston In January 2010, we started rehearsing for our Theatre tour. We worked eleven- or twelve-hour days learning routines and adapting our songs for live performance, so it was a crazy busy time, but we loved it. We were so excited about playing to a crowd who were there just to see JLS. On 26 January we performed our first show at the Rhyl Empire Theatre. It was fantastic and the fans went wild. That night and every single night after that, the energy of the fans just blew us away. All the venues were sold out and packed to capacity.

We had so much fun on that tour – we loved life on the road, and we still do. Everything about touring was new and exciting, from watching TV on the tour bus to hanging out with our dancers. The best thing about it was connecting with our fans. It was amazing to be able to meet them, play for them and thank them for everything they were doing for us – they have always been so brilliant, the best fans a band could ever have. They were there to meet us everywhere we went – at our hotels, concert venues and even service stations along the way. We were so grateful to them for the atmosphere they created at the gigs every night: it was always electric, always exhilarating.

When I look back on that tour, it's a blur. Recently, I went to see my mum and dad and nan and granddad at my granddad's house. While I was there, Granddad put on the Theatre tour. 'I love this,' he said, sitting back in his chair.

'Look how different I am then, how different I look,' I thought. It was almost like watching someone else on the screen. 'I remember being there but I don't remember doing any of it.'

It's very strange what happens to me when I'm on stage. As soon as I'm there, it's like a blackout. If I have a mic in my hand, I'll chat the most amount of rubbish, apparently. That's what the others tell me! I just let it happen. It's amazing to watch it back and I'm so lucky to have a record of it, but it's hard to understand why I can't remember any of it. It's always been the same, ever since we started. I can remember the crowd and the atmosphere, but when I come off stage, I never have a clue what I've been doing.

JB I didn't actually enjoy touring very much until our 2010 Summer tour, which took in places like Warwick Castle and Epsom Downs Racecourse. I loved performing, but we had to do a lot of promo in our time off during the Theatre tour and it was literally a 24-hour lifestyle. Doing shows, promotion and club appearances was hard work and very tiring. I'm known for liking my rest and if it was up to me, I'd probably be in bed half the time! Also, I felt frustrated because learning the choreography for the performances didn't come easily in the beginning. It infuriates me if I can't master something. We've had a lot of practice now and we're constantly learning new routines, so the whole process is a lot quicker, but that wasn't the case at the start of the first Theatre tour. I didn't like going on stage feeling less than 100 per cent confident with what I was doing; I hate making mistakes, especially if I know it's a mistake. When I know I'm not doing something right, it really upsets me. I couldn't enjoy touring to the full until I felt completely on top of my performance.

Marvin The start of 2010 was incredibly exciting for me, and not just because we were about to start on our first headline tour. The other reason was that two days into the New Year, I spoke to Rochelle Wiseman from The Saturdays and she told me she'd split up with her boyfriend. That was big news for me because I had liked Rochelle for the longest time.

I first met Rochelle when she interviewed me about being in the band VS on a BBC programme called *Smile*. She was sixteen, I was twenty and we were both in relationships. After that, I bumped into her here and there. I started seeing more of her when she joined The Saturdays because we were gigging on the same circuit and there was always chemistry between us. We instantly had a lot in common, but there was nothing I could do, even though I knew I liked her. I was single by then, but she was still in a relationship. So you can imagine how excited I was when I heard she had split up from her boyfriend. I waited for a few weeks before I asked her on a date and we started dating around the middle of February.

Touring and dating Rochelle coincided with the biggest highlight of our career, when we won two BRITs at Earls Court on 16 February: Best Breakthrough Act and Best British Single for 'Beat Again'. As well as being one of the most fantastic nights of my life, it was a turning point for the band because winning two of the most important awards in British music and being recognised by our peers finally started to set us apart from our *X Factor* association. There is no higher musical accolade in our country and it's something I'd dreamt of ever since I was a kid. It was a night of pure joy and happiness.

The BRITs is definitely the biggest night on the music calendar in the UK and to win not one, but two awards in front of all of our peers was just amazing. It was hard to believe it was happening and I felt so proud because it was such an incredible achievement. I kept thinking, 'We started this from nothing and now the four of us are standing here on stage in front of the world winning two massive awards.' It was the stuff dreams are made of, and a really wonderful feeling.

JB When you look at the press pictures from that night and you see our faces, we were over-the-moon happy, just completely elated. I know it's probably a bold claim, but I'm going to make a guess that there weren't any individuals as happy as we were that night.

My most prized possession is our BRIT for Best British Single for 'Beat Again'. It is incredibly special because the single was a collective effort and there are so many people who should be commended and congratulated for the award. Steve Mac and Wayne Hector, who wrote and produced the song, have probably written a hundred number ones between them, let alone all their countless Top 10 hits and number one albums, yet the 'Beat Again' BRIT Award is the only Best British Single they've won, until now. Considering their legacy, it's definitely saying something about how great the song is and how right it was for JLS.

It was an incredible night, a whirlwind night. At the afterparty, Jay-Z sent us over a bottle each of his personal champagne brand, Ace of Spades. I drank practically the whole bottle. Chloe was with me, as was my cousin Marc, who had originally encouraged me to get into the music business. They both had a glass, but I drank the rest.

Obviously the boys and I go out and drink, but we generally don't drink to excess, except when we're celebrating. We have never fallen out of clubs, or if we have, it hasn't been a regular occurrence. Yet that night I probably had so much to drink that I shouldn't have been able to move. We drank wine at the table as we watched the show and had drinks backstage after we won the awards, so I had been drinking all night, but what's funny is that I went home in the back of a car feeling stone-cold sober. I will never understand how that happened – I can only think that the adrenaline of the night overcame the effects of the alcohol. Either way, it was an incredible day and night, just unbelievable! I kept my Ace of Spades bottle (and the cork!) and the boys signed it, so it has pride of place in my house alongside the BRIT.

Oritsé When we performed at the BRITs, all I could think about was my mum and how much she had encouraged me when I was putting the band together. It was her belief in me that kept me going, along with my drive to be successful so I could help her, so I dedicated my performance to her.

It was a difficult time for me in many ways because we were doing so well and were so busy as a result that I wasn't getting to see my mum as much as I would have liked and I missed her. Our first tour sold out everywhere and took us all over the country until the middle of March. Every day off was spent writing or recording tracks for the second album, *Outta This World*.

After the success of the first album, which went on to sell 1.4 million units, people wondered whether we'd be able to pull it off again. That didn't worry me – I don't ever feel intimidated. From the beginning my approach to the whole game has been follow your instincts, follow your heart and be smart. If you worry about what hasn't happened yet, then it's going to drive you insane. I like doing things the natural way, the organic way – I really believe that everything is possible. Of course sometimes I have flashes of doubt, but for me it's important to be driven by determination and ambition, not concern and worry. I leave all the worry and the concern to anybody and everybody else. I don't have any time for that because I have to stay positive to be able to continue to work hard. All I ever try to do is be the best I can be. As long as I know I have done everything – I have pulled out all the stops and dug really deep to achieve my destined goals – then I'm satisfied.

JB Early in the year we went back into the studio with a view to releasing our second album at the end of 2010, which seemed like a reasonable amount of time to turn it around. We loved being in the studio; we loved writing. For us, it was a case of stepping up what we'd done on *JLS*. The first two singles on *JLS* had been written for us and we wanted to have more input on *Outta This World* so our main aims were to improve on our writing and vocals.

We had worked with some great people on the first album, like Steve and Wayne and Metrophonic, brilliant producers and writers who have been at the top of the industry for a very long time. We wanted to go on working with them, but we also wanted to extend our reach to more international producers, as well as develop our own songwriting. So after working on and off in London for the first few months of the year, in April we headed off to New York and LA to write most of *Outta This World*.

Apparently the second album is supposed to be difficult, but for me this was some of the best writing we had ever done in the studio. It definitely hit the tone and

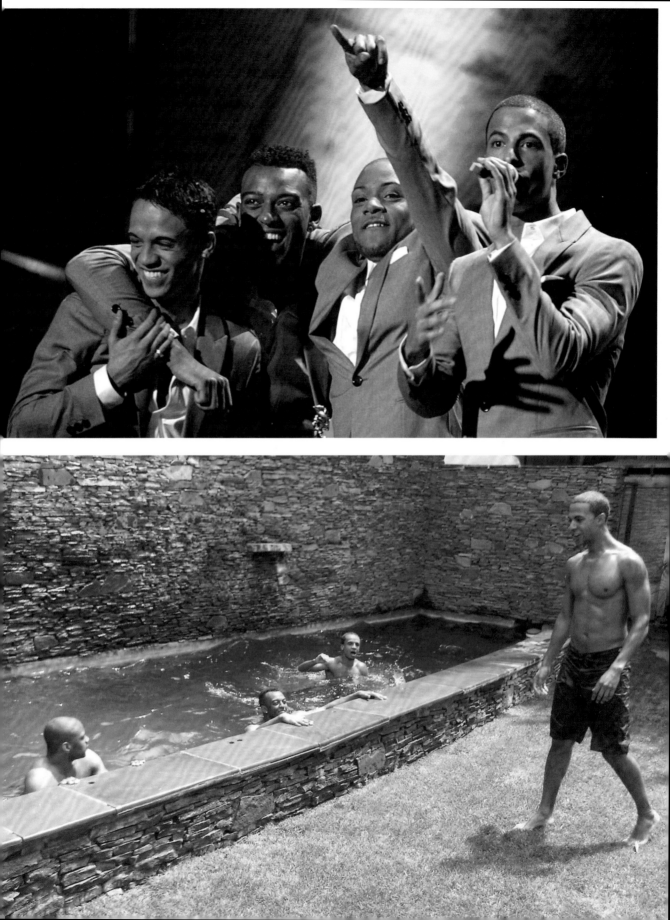

Outta This World will probably go down as one of our best albums. The first single, 'The Club Is Alive', isn't one of my favourites but when I first heard it I knew it was a single contender because it was so different, so off-the-cuff. The lyrics sample 'The Sound Of Music' from the musical of the same name and it was definitely an iconic song. Still, it could have been hit or miss. Luckily the gamble paid off and we had a number one with it.

Aston I wasn't intimidated; I was excited – 'Wow, we've got the chance to do another album!' It was brilliant that people had enjoyed our first album and as a result we had the opportunity to make music for a second album. The success of the first album meant there were people wanting to work with us beyond our wildest dreams. 'One of the writer-producers on the last Michael Jackson album, *Invincible*, wants to do a song for you guys,' our management told us.

When you hear that, you think, 'Flippin' heck– that's a bit mad!'. People who had worked with some of the greats over the years now wanted to work with us. That's just one of the reasons we approached the album with a feeling of pure excitement. Anyway, everything is a first for us. You can only ever make your second album once, and that makes it exciting.

My favourite JLS song ever is 'I Know What She Likes', a very old-school R&B track on *Outta This World*. It's easy to visualise what's happening in the lyrics. You picture yourself giving all these expensive gifts to a girl but she doesn't want material things – she prefers simple love notes or flowers. The concept is very romantic, but it definitely works and I think it would have been an amazing single. Either way, it sounded brilliant on the album.

JB I couldn't live in LA but I love working there. It's not the kind of place I would like to live because it's a place to work, a working centre, and not somewhere you can really relax. I'm aware that's a broad generalisation because LA is a big county and California is a huge state, but it strikes me that living there would be too much for me, especially as I don't really like the constantly busy vibe of Hollywood. I guess I'm the same when it comes to London – I would like the luxury of having a place in town, but I would never live in town because it's good to step outside of the hustle and bustle. I'm the type of person who likes to chill out at the weekend, go for walks in the park and spend time with my family. I'm sure there are places in LA where you can do all of that stuff, but I guess I haven't experienced it because I've spent all my time in hotels around Hollywood.

Hollywood is a great place to work, though. The sun is shining almost every day and the studios are brilliant. You tend to think of a recording studio as a small dark room with no windows, with machines whirring all day, but there is so much land in LA that the studios have big, airy, light rooms and swimming pools. It's incredible because you can come out of a room after playing the piano and delivering your vocals and dive straight into a pool. I would happily work out there for three or four months a year if I needed to.

Our studio sessions usually started around midday, so we could get up and do some shopping if we wanted to, go and see some sights or just sit by the pool and have a late breakfast. No prizes for guessing that I was the one who always got up late and ate my breakfast poolside! We'd finish in the studio between six and eight and then either go back to the hotel and have dinner there, just the four of us, or go out with some of the writers or producers we were working with. After dinner, we often went out to a club. One of the perks of being an artist is that you can get into clubs and go to places that you perhaps wouldn't be able to if you were away on holiday and didn't know anyone.

A big highlight of being in LA is the food. The hotels we stayed in had some really good restaurants and there was a Western-style place on Sunset Boulevard we often went to, where the ribs were the best I've ever had – we called it the Rib Shack, but that wasn't its real name. We saw Hugh Hefner there once, surrounded by *Playboy* bunnies. What I love about LA is that there are famous people everywhere. It's unique in that way – you just don't see it in other countries, or not to the same extent. Although there are paparazzi, they're not as full-on as they are in the UK. Everyone goes to Sunset for meetings because it's the central hub of the industry, so people are used to seeing Eva Longoria or Will Smith walking past. They expect it, so it's not a big deal to them. I'll never forget the time Britney Spears walked past Oritsé and me in our hotel restaurant, though. She was totally on her own, without any security, and there was no hassle, no drama, no hype surrounding her – we couldn't believe our eyes!

We worked with Wayne Hector and Toby Gad on 'Love You More', the second single from the album. 'Love You More' is a huge song, a beautiful song. It's a favourite of mine because I co-wrote it. It was surreal how it came together at Toby Gad's studio in LA. Marvin, Wayne, Toby and I were working together that day. We'd tried writing a couple of songs earlier in the day, but we weren't getting the vibe and nothing was really working so we all took a break and Toby went for a swim in the pool in his studio. After he dried off, he sat at the piano and started playing some chords.

'What is that?' we asked instantly. 'You need to put that into the computer! We are going to start writing to it now.' We began writing there and then and everything fell into place to create a brilliant song. A guy called Sanja directed the 'Love You More' video, which we shot later in the year at various locations including Venice Beach. It was designed to be very authentic, with a home video vibe, even though it has a very glossy feel to it. It was beautifully directed and I love everything about it. Despite it going to number one, though, I think the single was underrated if you compare it to our highest-selling singles.

Marvin *Outta This World* is my favourite album, for sure. The first album is great, but it was incredibly exciting to go to America and work with Stargate and other producers. We collaborated with some really great people. It was exciting to be in the studio again because we were rolling on a high off the back of a massive album that had sold a phenomenal number of units. It sold more than 230, 000 copies in the first week alone and was the fastest selling album of the year. It went on to sell 1.4 million copies. That kind of success can intimidate people, but we always knew that we would do OK if we just continued to do what we enjoyed doing, experimenting with different sounds and pushing our vocal and lyrical skills.

Making the second album has great memories for me because we had so much fun, especially in New York and LA. We were still doing a lot of promo, but there was also time to go partying in the evenings and go to the gym or do a bit of shopping in the morning because we didn't have to get to the studio until 2 p.m. or 3 p.m. or 4 p.m. It was quite relaxed and easy, and I think that's often when your best work comes. The great thing about the four of us is that we can write as a pair, as a threesome, all together or by ourselves – we all want the best. We all want to go to the others and say, 'I've written this,' and for the others to say, 'Wow, that's amazing!'

It was a huge honour to be asked to release the BBC Children in Need single for 2010 and we chose 'Love You More'. Even now when I perform 'Love You More', I get goosebumps feeling the lyrical content and the message. We wanted to achieve universality with it when we wrote it, but for me it was also inspired by my feelings for Rochelle – I always think about her when I sing it. Our fans were the other main inspiration because every day we love our fans a little bit more, so it works on more than one level.

When we recorded it, Nick Raphael, who was the head of our label at the time, called it a 'career record'. I didn't understand what he meant then but I understand now. 'Love You More' is a timeless song that will continue to be played and remembered for a long time to come. Along with 'Everybody In Love', it will form part of the JLS legacy. For me, both of these songs have more of a classic, universal appeal than 'Beat Again' and 'She Makes Me Wanna', which came later. 'Everybody In Love' and 'Love You More' are the big, anthemic numbers when we do live shows.

Aston Every time you hear a new song, however much you like it yourself, you always have a little bit of doubt in your mind about it. So when it came to 'Love You More', I sensed that it was a special song, but would other people agree? Having it selected for the Children in Need song confirmed my belief in it and the response to it when it was released was amazing.

As much as you love a song, you know that you can't get emotionally attached to it until everyone agrees that it's as good as you think it is. You could be playing it to yourself for weeks after you record it, thinking, 'I love this song so much!' and then your label could turn round to you and say, 'That's absolute rubbish,' and that's the end of it.

It's a collaborative and strategic decision, so it's not just about whether you like it. To be fair, whenever the four of us agree on a song, then we're onto a winner. It's rare for it to happen, but it was the case with 'Everybody In Love' and 'She Makes Me Wanna'.

Marvin My favourite video is probably 'Love You More'. Filmed in LA in black and white, it is beautifully shot and we had a great time making it, although to be fair we had a great time whenever we went to LA to shoot videos or record albums.

It always reminded us of how far we had come from the early days of the band, when we could only dream about working with great American producers and directors. With 'Love You More', the director caught the mood of the song in a way that was natural, organic and believable and yet it has a really classy finish to it. It's a huge favourite with our fans.

'Love You More' was the first song we wrote that went to number one – on 21 November 2010. It's a fantastic song with a beautiful message, made 100 per cent more special because it was the Children in Need single. We are fortunate because we have been involved in several charity singles, including the *X Factor* single 'Hero' and 'Everybody Hurts' for Help For Haiti. We've had great success with charity singles, none more so than 'Love You More'. I suppose historically charity singles have always been a bit tongue-in-cheek and fun, but I think we flipped that on its head with 'Love You More', which is a soulful ballad – it just worked.

Oritsé Right from the start, one of our ambitions was to work with different charities. Our success with the first singles and album put us in a position to raise money and awareness for different causes and we jumped on the chance to give something back. Marvin became an ambassador for the National Society for the Prevention of Cruelty to Children – or NSPCC – and JB chose to support Rays of Sunshine, which is a charity that grants wishes mainly for children living with chronic illnesses or terminal disease. Aston supports Beat Bullying and I chose the Multiple Sclerosis Foundation because my mum has MS.

I'm very involved with the MS Society now. I've put my efforts into doing as much as I can with them, getting involved in fundraising for research to find a cure. Hopefully one day we will be able to find a cure. I desperately hope that it will be in time to help my mum.

I am also very involved with helping and supporting young carers. When I was caring for my mum as a teenager, I thought I was the only person in this situation. I didn't realise that I wasn't alone – I had no idea that there are hundreds of thousands of young carers all over the country. Now I try my best to make sure I do as much as I can to help, inspire and influence young carers by reaching out, talking to them, listening to them and sharing experiences. It's very important to me.

Marvin Over the last five years, we've done stuff that people can only dream about and very few people will experience. With it comes fame and money, but also responsibility because we are effectively role models to some people.

Fame has its ups and its downs. For me, the ups massively outweigh the downs. You can count the downsides to fame on one hand. One of them is not being able to spend as much time with loved ones as you want to, because you have to be in another country or you're on tour. That can be hard but a lot of people have to make similar kinds of sacrifices for their work, so it's not a unique problem. Being interrupted or asked for photographs and autographs while you're out isn't always easy, but I take it with a pinch of salt. I know I have a famous face and as a result people are going to ask me for photographs or stop me in the street for autographs. It's part of what I do. I can understand why some people can't handle it, but I'm fine with it. Maybe it's because of my age and experience or perhaps it's a personality thing, but I just get on with it. When it comes to fame, I'm not going to be one of those people who proclaim themselves to be hard done by – I think that's a bit excessive.

The way I see it, we've been given an opportunity of a lifetime. Well, whether we have been given the opportunity, earned it or worked for it, I believe in Karma and I believe in fate. I believe in good things happening to good people and if good things happen to you, it's important to give back. In order for the world to go round, you just can't keep taking all the time. I see it as the circle of life: you have to give to keep it spinning. I know the boys share the same ethos – we try to give back as much as we take from this world, and that includes time as well as money. We are in the fortunate position of being able to make a life-changing difference to people by meeting them and spending time with them, so we do it as much as we can.

JB The only way to do charity is not to publicise it. Charity is about giving, and giving what you can give; it's not just giving for the sake of giving and it includes things that are difficult to give. When people run a marathon, climb a mountain, or do a skydive for charity, they are usually making a sacrifice, whether it be facing a fear of heights or pushing the boundaries of their health.

Our success means that we are able to touch people in a particular way. It means we are in a position to raise money and help out financially, but it also gives us the chance to lift people's spirits when they are ill or having a tough time. We can make a huge difference by visiting someone in hospital – we've been told that people have become so much better after seeing us for just fifteen minutes or half an hour. For us, that is priceless.

People ask us if it's hard doing hospital visits, but it's always nice to offer someone a bit of light relief when they're feeling low. Ill people are like anybody else – it's just that they are going through something that is very difficult. Often the last thing you want to do when you go through that difficulty is talk about it, so we chat about the fun things, things we can laugh about – 'What's the food like?' Whenever you go into someone's room, you can instantly see what interests them, so there are always points to talk about. For instance, we'll go into a young boy's room, he may be twelve and a fan of JLS, or he might not be much of a fan but he has Manchester United posters on his wall. I'll laugh about how I don't like Manchester United because I'm an Arsenal fan. Then I'll tease Marvin for liking Chelsea and we'll talk about how Oritsé doesn't support anyone. Often we sing something. It's amazing how a few bars of 'Everybody In Love' can lift the mood and the spirit.

People always ask us, 'Are you role models?' I say, 'Well yes, everybody in the world, whether they like it or don't like it, is a role model.'

At the end of the day, whoever you are, there is always someone who is less well-off than you and you can make a change to their life. It may be that you happen to have a bit more influence, a bit more reach, because you're well known and people look up to you, but everybody can help someone who is less well-off than they are. For me, it is one of our duties as human beings to be able to fulfil that role.

★ ★ ★ ★

Far and Wide

We were busier than we'd ever been and the band had to come first, which meant that some of our personal relationships faltered, were put on hold, or didn't even get off the ground. In the summer of 2010, we did a six-week US tour and made our first attempts to break the US market. For one reason or another we didn't make the impact we were hoping for, which was disappointing. But back in the UK, we started gearing up for a massive arena tour and won our third and fourth MOBO awards, an incredible honour. Tinie Tempah featured on 'Eyes Wide Shut', the third single from 'Outta This World' and guested at some of our arena shows. The tour began in late November and sold out all around the country. The response from our fans was literally mind-blowing. We had the time of our lives...

JB Chloe and I had a turbulent patch around the time JLS were making the second album because she was based at home and I was running around the world. We were so busy – we were here, there and everywhere. Our Theatre tour finished in early March 2010 and after that we were back and forth to LA and New York, doing promo and going into the studio to write and record. In June and July we played all over the UK and Ireland.

When I look back at the schedule, it was crazy. One day we performed on *Britain's Got Talent*, the next we flew by private jet to Dublin to support Westlife in front of 80,000 people at Croke Park, which was another huge highlight of 2010. The day after that we played the Capital Summertime Ball in London and two days later, we were back in America for six days of promo. The following week we packed in two days in Ireland performing, a day at the Isle of Man Festival, a gig at Haydock Park Racecourse in Merseyside and three days in Canada!

Aston To concentrate 100 per cent on what we wanted to do, we had to leave a lot behind. We had to put friendships and relationships on hold; we even had to put our health on hold – get less sleep, relax less and just go all out, physically and mentally.

I didn't have a girlfriend for three to four years after my last long-term girlfriend I was with. For me, it wasn't the right time to be in a relationship because I was travelling so much and our schedule was crazy busy. So when I met Sarah, a dancer, at the Summertime Ball, I was happy with just being friends. I liked her immediately, but I didn't really think about it because she had a boyfriend.

It is always flattering when girls ask me to write their number down – 'Please call me!' In the early days of JLS, I often called those numbers. I had a brilliant time – I love women, they are amazing! Some of them went on to sell kiss and tells on me but that hasn't upset me. 'Whatever,' I think. 'It's fine. I do what I do, I did what I did – I learnt from it.' Since I was single, I didn't think there was any need for me to be particularly careful. If I'd had a girlfriend and was going around doing what I was doing, that would have been terrible.

I have lots of friends who are girls and Sarah and I stayed friends. I didn't have her number, but I saw her out and about and we got on. We'd always stop for a chat – 'How are you?' – it was all good. A year or so later, she was single for a while and we went out on a date to Covent Garden for a drink and dinner. Nothing really happened after that because I went off to America again and she was doing her own thing.

JB It's obviously hard for your family when you're away, but my mum and dad had accepted that I was going to leave home. It is what it is – it's all part of growing up. But it's different for a girlfriend, especially if she is at home, you're away and your time together is very limited. Chloe and I still had a lot to talk about because being a dancer she knew a lot of the people we were working with, but it was hard for her not being part of it. We nearly split up many times.

Even when I was at home, we didn't actually get to have a normal relationship because whenever we were out and about, people were always coming up to talk and ask for a photo. Most people were very polite about it, but it was hard at times because a normal couple wouldn't have those constant interruptions. It's one of the sides of fame that you don't foresee. Although it's brilliant to have people coming up and asking for your photo, it does affect your relationship and the vibe between you.

I wouldn't have changed anything, though because it was incredible to be travelling with Marvin, Aston and Oritsé and working with amazing songwriters and producers, especially once we had won the BRITs. We always had aspirations to go over to America and into other parts of the world, so it was amazing to have the chance to fulfill our dreams. I loved it.

In August, we did a US tour of Six Flags theme parks. The tour lasted for six weeks and we played all over the country, from Los Angeles to Chicago, to Atlanta. In between, we did bits of promo here and there, but nowhere near as much as we would have liked to do. If I'm going to be honest, I was upset at the amount of effort that was put into promotion on that trip. There were some great people at Jive, our American label. Justin Timberlake, Chris Brown, Usher, Britney and Backstreet Boys were just some of the artists on their roster, so it was a heavyweight label. Yet I don't think we were taken seriously enough by them to say that we did America properly. We worked with some really brilliant people day to day, but I think the powers that be at the label either didn't see the value of JLS or they didn't see us as contenders to break the US market.

For instance, when American acts do TV they always have a live band. We wanted a live band and we were told that we couldn't have one because of the budget restrictions enforced by the label. I'll never forget our first promo on a breakfast TV show. The sound was horrendous because we weren't allowed to use the sound guy who was travelling with us and the guy assigned to us that day didn't really know too much about it and didn't press hard enough to improve the sound quality. We are passionate about paying attention to every last detail, especially when it comes to our sound, so it was incredibly upsetting.

So we didn't have our own live band, we didn't have a sound check and we were in a foreign country. It was our first appearance in America and I could have cried as I watched it back. Two of the mics were too low and one was too high, so you couldn't really hear anything. We made the best of it because we try to make the best of every situation and we give everything to every performance. All sorts of elements affect your performance, including money, knowledge and experience, but even in the early days of club appearances and on the Lemar tour, we still performed to the best of our ability. Everything was on point, from styling to our routine, and we sounded as good as we possibly could. But now that we supposedly had the money, knowledge and experience to give a slick performance, we sounded terrible.

I brought it up with one of the top guys at the label when we had dinner with him the night afterwards. 'Did you see the performance on the breakfast show?' I asked him.

'I did, yeah,' he said.

'What did you think?'

'Well, you know, it wasn't the best, but there is always next time.'

That really, really upset me. Everybody knows that there is no next time, especially when you're trying to break a new market. You are only as good as your last performance, whether you're playing rugby or singing with a band. I thought his answer was so insulting.

Yet in terms of experience, the Six Flags tour is probably the best tour I've ever done because there were no distractions. There was nothing else going on, we were devoted to performing. It was like going back to the beginning of JLS, when nobody knew us and we had to build up a following. It was a challenge and we all love a challenge, which is why we worked so hard when we formed the band.

We did some great shows in America. One show was in Rochester, New York, where one of my uncles was living. He was my mum's brother. Because of the distance between us, we hadn't seen each other much but I had great memories of him and his family coming to stay with us in Brixton a couple of summers in a row when I was at primary school. We were living in a big Victorian house with a cellar and an attic, so it was a great place to hang out with my cousins all summer. They were the best summers of my childhood.

I'd never been over to Rochester, so it was great to be able to call my uncle and say, 'Yes, I'm here.' I invited the whole family to the show and the boys and I went bowling with them afterwards. It was such a great thing to be able to show my uncle what I was doing now. He didn't know much about JLS or the scope of our fame in the UK, and we were able to hang out in a bowling alley with no hassle whatsoever. We had a brilliant time. It was really lovely and I treasure the memory, because sadly my uncle recently passed away from cancer.

We did other shows in America, not in the major areas like New York and LA, but in quieter places, where people like Selena Gomez were on the bill. We were the support act, the underdogs, and we took it all in our stride – we were there to make an impression and we relished the challenge. We went all out to make it an enjoyable time for the audience, even though they had come to see Selena. I don't remember if we met her. Of course if I'd known then what I know now, I would obviously have said hi and had a photo and all the rest of it. Back then I didn't have a clue who she was.

Aston There were a lot of things that didn't add up in America. We had a strong sense that we weren't being fully supported internationally – that was the main thing. If you don't have 100 per cent backing, it's not going to work, simple as that. Something should have happened for us in America because after selling the number of albums we did with JLS, our first album, and after creating the kind of hysteria we did, it made sense for people in the US to be saying, 'Have you heard this from the UK?'

Sometimes I wonder if we would have done better if we'd just tried to do it ourselves, rather than let other people organise us. I think we would have made much more progress because we are so on it. If somebody gives us a lead, two weeks later one of us is emailing back to say, 'What is happening with this?' Nothing slips us by. That's because as much as this is our business, it is our lives as well.

We really wanted our music to be released in the US. If you try and it doesn't work, that is fine. At least you tried. If you don't try, it's frustrating to be getting messages from people on the other side of the world, saying, 'Just seen your stuff online, love it'.

When those messages turn into a hundred and then a thousand and keep on multiplying, you want to say, 'Please release the album! It's very clear that people want to hear it.' If you miss that window of opportunity the first time, it's always going to be harder the next time.

In my mind, releasing an album in a new territory means doing everything you can to promote it, including a radio tour, TV shows, posters everywhere, just everything. In America, we did a couple of radio events, we did a couple of TV shows – it was a drop in the ocean. We went there ready to work and they didn't put us to work enough. The Six Flags tour was great but it wasn't fully promoted. It's all well and good us doing a tour, but when you have no more than two hundred people coming to watch, it's a bit like, 'Cool, I know everything starts with one person and spreads by hearsay, but we are only over here for a limited time and we need to work quickly to capitalise on our UK success.'

As a band, we are very proactive. We are never reactive and we never were. Fair enough, we travelled across the country and went to three states in one day. That's really cool, but what did we actually do in that time? I'd rather have stayed in one state and done fifteen TV shows. It's all well and good spreading it out, but it wasn't well enough coordinated and I don't think the belief was really there.

I had a lot of hope for America and I don't think it really clicked in with us that it wasn't going to happen in the US territory until a year after the tour. Then we decided, 'You know what, let's just forget it and work on what we've got going on here. Let's just keep on doing what we do in the UK. If it happens in America, it happens. If not, cool!'

Oritsé Whether we made it in America wasn't down to us. It was an issue of politics and I'm not afraid to talk about it. During that time I saw another side to the business. I realised that it's more than just what you do as a person and your determination. We are the hardest-working band in the business and we were geared up to go all out in the US. So, why didn't it happen? There were a number of factors that didn't allow us to progress.

There are the people who push the buttons and if they don't push enough buttons, then there is nothing you can really do. As the trip unfolded, I thought, 'This is a new experience.' Until then, it had been a smooth ride for us to the top of our game. This was the first time we experienced a bump in the road. 'OK, it's a bump,' I thought. 'We can always come back and try again.'

People have said, 'It wasn't your time' and 'Maybe it was too early' but I think it was also political: it was business. The music industry isn't about making friends, it's about making money; everyone has to succeed and if someone else's project has to succeed at the expense of your project, then people make that decision. It's not as if they don't like you as people, they just want to win. If it looks like you're going to stop them from winning for some reason, they don't mind easing off to push something else forward. It's like chess and I could instantly see it for the game it was. Still, it's a real shame because our music couldn't have been more suited for America. The first *JLS* album was ideal for the market and *Outta This World* was an amazing album, specifically directed at America.

Of course, everyone found it disappointing that things didn't happen for us there, but I've been through worse in my life so I wasn't devastated. I just thought, 'I can see what is happening and I'm going to take this experience and use it.' Difficult situations like that can't defeat me. I've experienced many scenarios that could have defeated me, but they haven't. It's a pattern in my life. Something that baffles people about me is that negativity doesn't touch me. I think it's because nothing could be worse than my mum being unwell and having to fight for her and my family. If I can survive that, then I can survive anything.

So the American tour was just another experience that I found interesting and learnt from. It was the same when I was mentoring AJ's band Vida and we were supposed to break through, but certain elements of the business didn't allow it. In my time I've learnt two sides of the business because I've done things inside and outside of the band, on a business level as well as an artist's level. I've seen two sides of the game and that has made me much stronger as a person moving forward for what I'm going to do in the future.

I fully realise that it's a music *business* and there are a number of factors that give you a result. It's not just about your talent – there are lots of talented people who don't break through. You have to make sure that you tick all the right boxes. Behind the scenes, the industry is a different world to the one you witness when you watch an artist or a band performing on the TV and think they made it there purely on merit.

JB When we came back from America, we went straight into a whirlwind of promo for *Outta This World*, which was due to be released in November 2010. We did photo shoots and press interviews. We appeared on chat shows on radio and TV, including *Paul O'Grady*, *Celebrity Juice*, *Never Mind the Buzzcocks* and a JLS ITV special. We were also gearing up for our first arena tour, where we'd be taking our performance to another level and playing to audiences of 14,000 people every night. This tour was to be another step up from the Theatre tour and we wanted to make it extra special for the fans.

We worked very closely with our creative director on the tour concept – we wanted to do something spectacular, to put on a show that went beyond the fans' expectations and left them with a real wow feeling. The concert started with a drive-in cinema vibe when we entered the arena in a car that was suspended from the ceiling. Arriving through the air meant we were able to travel right across the auditorium, connecting with all the different sections of the arena while we sang our opening song. I can't express how amazing it felt to look down at all those happy faces – it was one of the best feelings in the world! It felt fantastic to be making so many people happy.

It was really important to involve each and every person in our performance. We wanted to be as close to our fans as possible, even though we were playing at huge venues. Later on in the show we performed on walkways that took us right into the crowd. That was so special and it definitely made the whole experience far more intimate for everyone.

Just over a month before the tour started, we travelled to Liverpool for the MOBOs 2010. That was another incredible night. When it came to our music, one of the things we contended with was our ability to cross over between pop music and the urban music world, so it was amazing to win our third and fourth MOBOs that year, for Best UK Act and Best Album. Yes, we'd stepped up from winning Best Newcomer in 2009 to being recognised as established artists only twelve months later. It was unbelievable to win the top award for the *JLS* album – it was a credit to the people we'd worked with, a credit to us and a credit to MOBO for recognising us. We felt very honoured.

We've had a lot of support and love from MOBO and we have only missed one MOBO Awards in four years, because we were rehearsing for the Michael Jackson tribute concert in Cardiff. It is very important for us to support the MOBOs and their founder Kanya King, who has achieved great things in music and in the industry. MOBO has definitely transformed music in the UK – you only have to look at how urban music has dominated the charts for the last few years to see its impact.

On 22 November, we released *Outta This World* and it went double platinum within a month and a half. We were slightly disappointed that it went in at number two below Take That's album *Progress*, but the sales figures were brilliant and musically, we were very proud of the album. November was crazy for us – we were rehearsing intensively for the tour while squeezing in as much album and tour promo as we could. Then, a week after the album was released, we embarked on our first sell-out arena tour.

Marvin Our first night was at the Aberdeen AECC on 29 November. I vividly remember seeing this sea of lights and people smiling, yelling and singing along. It was the best feeling to be up there and quite unbelievable! As I looked round at my three mates, I couldn't help thinking, 'Is this really for us?' We had the time of our lives on that tour. It was brilliant being on the road together and we loved every minute of performing the shows.

We wore coloured hoodies in the last section of the show, just like we used to back in the day. I was in green, JB was in yellow, Oritsé was in red and Aston's was blue. I loved those outfits – they made me feel nostalgic for the days when we'd all sing acapella round one microphone in front of a cheering club crowd at 1 a.m. They reminded me of how far we had come.

JB The fans loved it when we sang 'Eyes Wide Shut'. Their reaction to it live was incredible and they knew all the words, so we decided to release it as our third single. When we finished the remix, we thought it would be great to have a feature artist. We'd wanted to work with Tinie Tempah for a while, so we sent it over to him to see what he thought. His career was blowing up at the time, but he loved it and was really happy to rap on the single. It went from there and the rest, as they say, is history. The remix would definitely have been a number one single had it been released before the album, but it still did really well.

Aston Everything about this whole industry is so strategically planned that you need to be 100 per cent confident that you're making the right decision when you select an album track or single. When we were going through the selection process for the second album, 'Eyes Wide Shut' was a little bit overlooked at first. It was a bit of a dark horse – there were so many songs in our heads and I suppose you could say that we were spoilt for choice. We didn't realise we had such a good track already written and recorded, then suddenly everyone seemed to love it.

JB 'Eyes Wide Shut' is one of my favourite songs and it's my favourite video, full stop. It was the sixth video we made but our first green-screen shoot, which meant that we filmed our performances in a studio against a blank canvas and all the special effects and graphics were added later. It was mind-blowing to perform with only a concept in mind – we really didn't know how it was going to turn out. It was perfect when we saw it. None of us wanted any changes, which was a first for one of our videos. We watched the first edit and said, 'We like that.' That was that, it was done.

Marvin If I'm honest, I find green-screen videos quite boring to shoot. You can't really get into the zone or the character of the video because you are literally doing everything in front of a green screen. The director tells you about all this amazing, crazy stuff that is going to happen but you don't see it so it's hard to know exactly what the result will be. Still, the end product is amazing and I loved the video after all the graphics were added. It was great to have Tinie Tempah featured on the video as well as the single because some featured artists don't want to get involved with the video. Tinie is a great guy. He comes from the area where I grew up and we have mutual friends, so it was brilliant that we could work with him.

Oritsé Tinie is a good friend now. He supported us on the London dates at the O2 and Wembley, which was amazing. His appearance on 'Eyes Wide Shut' really took things to another level – the fans went crazy when they saw him. He was there the night in January 2011 when we filmed the show for our 3D film, *Eyes Wide Open*, which mixed performance and documentary footage of the tour, along with interviews with each band member. That night was amazing, even though we were nervous about being filmed. Everything seemed to come together to make it one of the best shows we've ever performed.

The song I like to perform most is 'Everybody In Love'. It's just one of those songs that everyone just connects with – there isn't one person in the audience who doesn't know that song, who doesn't put their hands up and take part and get really involved. Everybody loves it and you can really feel the energy from the audience when you're performing it.

JB There were loads of highlights to our arena tour show. We treated every night like it was our first and tried to mix things up a bit. There were some great sections. I loved dressing up in a top hat and tails and getting into a 'haunted house' mood for the second section – it really appealed to the urban gentleman in me. The dance battle between us four and the girl dancers always worked really well, before we stripped things back to perform 'Umbrella'.

I was very excited the night we played the O2 for the first time. When I first met the boys, I said that we were capable of working with the top people in the industry and being signed by the top labels, so I always had 100 per cent belief that at some point we would get to the moment in our career when we headlined our own arena. Of course, I'm nervous before any first show – it doesn't matter where it is. I was nervous before our first theatre show and I was nervous before our first arena show in Aberdeen, but I was also excited and I was at one. I felt blessed to be there: it was meant to be.

It's important to us that everybody's happy on tour. We had the same dancers for the arena tour that we had used on the first tour. We all got on fantastically well during rehearsals and we worked very hard on our dancing because it makes the difference between seeing someone standing there delivering a great vocal performance and the wow of seeing a great show. We want people to feel they've really enjoyed themselves when they come away from a JLS concert.

Oritsé My experience of the tour was unique because nobody could share how I felt as I walked out on stage every night. Nobody saw what I went through to put the band together. Nobody saw the struggles I had with self-belief when people didn't believe in me. Nobody was aware that I was up having sleepless nights, working round the clock, looking for band members. So nobody could share how I felt when I looked out at twenty thousand people as we came out on stage to do our first arena show. 'Wow, so many people have come out to see the band I put together! It's mad,' I thought. None of the boys, not even my mum, could share that feeling.

My favourite memory from the arena tour is of driving up to the O2 Arena on the morning of our first show and seeing our name in lights: 'JLS PERFORMING LIVE!' For me this was a dream come true – I had envisioned and dreamed of that moment for a long time. It was also a turbulent day for me, though. One of my worst memories from the tour is sitting hidden in the corner of the car park alone just before we went on in the evening because my mum's health had taken a turn for the worse and I felt devastated. The more unwell she was becoming, the more helpless I felt. I wanted to help her so much, I wanted things to change for her but she wasn't getting better and that made me question a lot of things. 'Is the universe on my side or not?' I kept asking. I'd always thought it was, but why couldn't I help my mum?

I had thought that being successful was going to change my mum's life – I thought it would help her find a cure and make her life better and better. But that hasn't happened and her illness has meant that life has become more of a struggle for her. She has deteriorated over the last few years and I've found it hard to accept that I have no control over her illness; I haven't been able to make her better. I believe that anything is possible and I will always believe that, but it's not as easy as you might imagine when you are a kid and you assume that people get better at some point: some people don't get better.

After a while, I realised that I had to get myself together for the show. I spoke to my mum on the phone. 'You're about to perform in front of twenty thousand people,' she said. 'Get your head in the game and stay focused!'

My mum loves the band because it distracts me from the other things going on in my life. The great thing about being on stage is that nothing else matters while you're up there looking at people who have come to see you and support you in their thousands. That doesn't happen to most people and it makes me feel so fortunate, no matter what else is happening in my life. There's no greater feeling than having Marvin, JB and Aston, my boys, standing right next to me on that stage at the start of a show and thousands of fans screaming our names.

★ ★ ★ ★

In Different Worlds

In early 2011, we went back into the studio to start writing our third album, Jukebox. The first single from the album, 'She Makes Me Wanna' smashed it and became our fifth number one single. Needless to say, we all loved making the 'She Makes Me Wanna' video on the beach in Miami! We stepped things up even further and went on a solo stadium tour of the UK and performed with the Jackson Brothers at the Michael Jackson tribute concert in Cardiff, which was a dream fulfilled for all of us and one of the biggest concerts of our career. Two days later, we went to Uganda to film a series of reports for Sport Relief – an inspiring, troubling and very worthwhile trip.

JB After the tour ended on 29 January we had a short break to recharge our batteries. I went on holiday to Miami and then to Dallas to watch the Super Bowl. It was insane! I was with Chloe, my brother and Chloe's cousin, who is an American football fan. Marvin and Aston were in Miami while we were in Dallas, so we just missed them.

We spent most of March and April in the studio writing and recording our third album, *Jukebox*, in the UK, USA and Europe. *Jukebox* was probably our hardest album to deliver just because we were so up against it. Choosing the right singles and album tracks wasn't easy. Throughout 2011, we were crazy busy. We headlined more concerts than any other band in the UK and were crowned Hardest-working Band of the Year by PRS for Music, who keep a record of such things.

Our schedule and love of performing live put us under pressure during the making of *Jukebox*. We had committed ourselves to submit the album at the end of the year and it was a bit of a drama to get things done.

Marvin We took a break from writing to appear in what turned out to be a classic sketch for Comic Relief, 'Smithy to the Rescue', featuring all kinds of people, including Sir Paul McCartney, Ringo Starr, George Michael, Keira Knightley and Rio Ferdinand. We duetted with former Prime Minister Gordon Brown in the sketch, while Justin Bieber played keyboards – how mad is that? We were so proud to make a contribution to what is now seen as one of Comic Relief's funniest moments.

In May, we had a secret premiere for our 3D film *Eyes Wide Open*, which went on to break box-office records by making nearly half a million pounds in just one day. We were the first British music act ever to release a 3D film and it turned out to be the biggest music cinema event in UK history. On the first Friday in June it went on general release for one day only. Well, it was *meant* to be just one day, but some cinemas extended the run over the weekend because the demand for tickets was so overwhelming. It sold out all over the country and there were queues round the block.

We loved the film when we first saw it. The concert footage of our first arena tour is really spectacular. I love the moment when Tinie Tempah comes out onto the stage and the fans go mad. Taking you right back to the beginning of JLS, it's a nicely balanced portrait of the band, with tour footage, early videos, behind-the-scenes insight and some really heartfelt interviews.

JB 'She Makes Me Wanna' was the standout single and so we decided to make it the first release and started thinking about having a featured vocalist on the track. We'd been hoping to work with Rihanna for a while, but as you can imagine it was very difficult to lock her down to anything. Then Nick Raphael suggested Dev. Her song 'Booty Bounce' had been sampled on Far East Movement's massive worldwide hit 'Like A G6' and her career was blowing up at the time.

'Absolutely! We love what she is about. Let's do it,' we said.

Marvin After having Tinie on 'Eyes Wide Shut', it felt fresh to have a female featured artist this time around. Dev is a really cool girl and there was a real buzz around her at the time. She jumped on the track and did a great job; it really worked. She also came to Miami to shoot the video. You never know how a featured artist is

going to be when you work with them. Will they act like a diva on the video shoot? Will they agree to shoot the video in the first place? Some artists don't even agree to turn up. So it was great that Dev was a fun person and fully involved in the process. We really enjoyed working with her.

Aston It's not hard to imagine why the 'She Makes Me Wanna' video is a firm favourite of mine. Being a boy band member in my early twenties and single at the time, there I was filming a beach party video in the middle of Miami Beach with half-dressed women everywhere! For me, the vibe of the video captures JLS 100 per cent.

In the solo shots of me singing on the rocks, I was supposed to have a T-shirt on. 'Let's try it with the T-shirt off,' the director said, so I'm topless for most of the video.

Oritsé In June and July, the performance side of our work stepped up even further when we went on a solo stadium tour of the UK, headlining gigs with audiences of twenty-five thousand people and more. We started at the Hull KC Stadium and played at Winchester, Swindon, Alton Towers, Belfast, Limerick, Edinburgh, Newcastle and Milton Keynes, among others. It was great being able to reach so many fans in such a short space of time. The energy of our fans is something else – it has to be seen, heard and felt to be believed.

Aston We love performing, we love touring and until July 2011 we had never missed a gig. In fact, the only time we've ever pulled out of a commitment was at T4 on the Beach on 10 July 2011. I instigated it because we weren't happy.

T4 on the Beach was one of the first big gigs we ever did – we did it for two years in a row and it was incredibly exciting. We loved it and we put a lot of time and effort into it. But the third year we were asked to appear there, we were on our stadium tour. It was a real disappointment to have to say, 'We can't do it. We would love to but it's physically going to kill us.' The only way we were going to be able to get there in time would be to fly because we had a late show the night before.

The promoters bent over backwards – 'We will fly you over and get you here early in the morning in time for your sound check.'

Fine. We decided to give 'She Makes Me Wanna' its televised debut as part of our set, to make it special. So on the morning of the concert, we got up ridiculously early, got on a plane and arrived at the venue just before 8 a.m. On the posters outside, it said that the gates would open around 10 a.m. Olly Murs had his sound check before us. He was on stage at 8 a.m., bang, all went to plan. We were next up.

T4 on the Beach is a notoriously difficult gig to play because the sound doesn't bounce back – it just goes out onto the beach. As a result, whatever you can hear in your ear monitors is a beat ahead of whatever is playing and what everybody else can hear. I perform with one ear in and one ear out, so I need a sound check to get it right, especially as our dancers hear everything a beat behind us. At about 8.55 a.m., we went through our dance routines. Then we started into 'Everybody In Love'. About twenty seconds into the song, a horde of people started running through the gates. 'Hey, that's not right,' I thought. 'The gates don't open for another hour.'

At 9.30 a.m. we were taken off stage because we couldn't sound check our show and do our performance in front of the audience; it just wasn't going to happen. 'We are really sorry, there is nothing we can do,' the organisers told us. 'Everyone is running in now. The gates are open.'

'OK, but where does that leave us?' we said.

'You'll be fine, you'll be fine.'

'Hold on,' we said. 'We haven't done this version of the song before because we do it differently on tour. You want an exclusive and we are giving you an exclusive. We need a sound check.'

We went back to the dressing room. 'How do you feel? What do you want to do?' we asked each other. We quickly realised there were two options, and neither of them was very appealing: we knew the performance would be horrendous if we went ahead without a sound check, so either we didn't do the show or we did it badly. Which would be more detrimental to us? Well, much as we hated the idea of pulling out, doing a bad show would be even worse because people would be put off coming to see us live and that would affect the tour. Why would they want to come and see us live after seeing us perform a terrible set?

Our approach is always to be very accommodating, to give interviews and let people film behind the scenes. It's never a problem for us to give everyone access to the band but if, for whatever reason, something isn't professional, we don't want to do it. It wasn't just one gig, it was our career, and we were three years into it, with four number ones and several awards to our name – it felt like we weren't being treated very well.

So we said, 'Since you can't physically move people off that beach and we need a sound check, we are not going on.'

Then it was announced that, 'JLS have pulled out of the show.'

We had to accept that we were going to be seen as bad guys for a while. Still, we knew that when it was time for us to have our say, we'd have our say. Until then, we just had to take it on the chin – 'OK, cool. We are not doing the show'. Luckily, our old friend Alan Carr asked us all about it three days later and we were able to explain a bit more about the situation.

We have learnt that anything to do with JLS, even if it only involves the JLS team, is always going to affect the four of us and the JLS brand; we get that. And when stuff does happen, we will take it on the chin until we are asked what really happened.

For us, the whole T4 disaster was overshadowed by the release of 'She Makes Me Wanna' on 24 July 2011. The record went straight in at number one. It was our fifth number one and we were over the moon. A week later, we went to LA and spent the whole of August writing and recording. It was as hot as can be that month, but we loved every minute – and every ray of sunshine – of that trip!

Marvin It's no secret that I am a massive Michael Jackson fan, as I'm sure most people in the music industry are. So it was incredible to get an email from our manager, saying, 'Something has come up that you guys are not going to believe. It's an opportunity to perform with The Jacksons at Michael's tribute concert, MJ Forever, in October.'

My mouth dropped open as I read those words. It was unbelievable to think we would be on the same stage as Michael's brothers, performing their hits. It didn't sink in for ages.

We were booked to rehearse at a studio in west London in late September. When we walked in, there was Jackie, Marlon and Tito Jackson, three of our childhood heroes, dancing around to 'Blame It On The Boogie' in tracksuit bottoms and hoodies. Wow, it was weird stepping into that to join them! It was just so incredibly surreal. These were people we had looked up to our entire lives. We had emulated, admired and adored them and now we were going to share a stage with them in celebration of the life of the greatest entertainer of all time.

It wasn't easy trying to hold it together. We didn't want to seem too much like the crazy fans we are because we were going to be performing together. Obviously we said how much we admired and respected them and how much of an honour it was to be taking part in the tribute concert, but since we wanted to make sure we put on the best performance ever, we quickly moved on to rehearsing because we had only a limited amount of time with them.

Together we went on to perform one of The Jacksons' biggest hits, 'Blame It On The Boogie', at the Cardiff Millennium Stadium on 8 October 2011. For the performance, we wore the same jackets as the Jackson brothers, with an armband that was a favourite with Michael. Afterwards, we performed 'The Way You Make Me Feel' by ourselves. It was just brilliant!

'The Way You Make Me Feel' had been a special song for us ever since we performed it in the second week of the X Factor finals. Back then, we were desperately trying to make it and it was the first time we introduced a dance routine into our performance. Now we were performing it on the world stage in front of Michael Jackson's mother and his children, along with Beyoncé and Christina Aguilera, who also played sets at the concert. It was a poignant moment for me, just thinking about how far we had come. It was also poignant because Michael Jackson was a hero to all of us and his death had saddened us all. Still, I tried not to think about any of this too much in case it made everything else a bit too nerve-wracking.

After years of performing as JLS we were used to learning dance routines, so we decided to copy Michael's dance moves for our performance of 'The Way You Make Me Feel'. Visually, I knew the moves off by heart because I've watched that video so many times in my life. I think it was the same for all of us. But it's one thing knowing a dance by sight and another to copy it accurately, so we were grateful that there was a choreographer on hand to teach us. We were learning to dance like Michael! It was really fun.

As always with this type of concert, it was a bit weird backstage. You'd think all the artists would get together in one room and catch up, but it's not like that. Everyone has their own dressing room and people pretty much keep themselves to themselves until they go on stage. As you wander around on your way to catering, the toilet or to the stage, Christina Aguilera passes you and Janet Jackson and Paris and Prince Michael walk by, but you don't really get to chat. It just adds to the surreal feeling surrounding the whole event, really.

It felt scary to be performing with my idols – it was crazy to be on stage with people I'd looked up to for my whole life. Suddenly we were on the same level, which was totally weird. They say you should never meet your idols, but in this case it was pure pleasure. The Jacksons were so great, so down-to-earth and so normal, despite being part of one of the most incredible success stories in pop history. They are still performing to this day and they are granddads. The next day each of the jackets we'd worn for the performance was framed. In the corner of each frame was a photo of us on stage with the Jackson brothers and in mine there was a picture of me singing with Jackie Jackson, with our arms around each other. That was an amazing sight. Imagine, performing with The Jacksons! For me, it was definitely one of the highlights of our career, 100 per cent. It's unbelievable what we have achieved.

I only wish I'd met Michael Jackson. He is the only person I never got to meet. Aston and I shared a flat for about eighteen months and we were together a lot of the time but the night Michael Jackson died was the first night Aston had ever stayed out. So I was in the house by myself for the first time and I started seeing the messages coming through that Michael Jackson had died. To begin with I thought it must be a hoax – most people did. Then it started to hit BBC and Sky that it was true. I was devastated. It didn't surprise anyone that he died but it did shock people, and I was the same. It was one of those weird times. Firstly, I was very upset that he passed away in those circumstances and secondly, it meant that I would never get to meet him. It was a real shame and such a waste.

He's the only person I wish I'd met, though I feel like I've met everybody else, from Stevie Wonder to Beyoncé and Mariah Carey. For me the best was meeting Stevie Wonder. He is really cool, a really nice guy.

Just before we bumped into him, we were sitting in the lounge at Heathrow Airport about to board a flight to LA in 2010. It was about two in the morning and over breakfast, the four of us were having a little debate about who was the best singer in the world. I said I thought it was the R&B singer Brian McKnight.

'Yes, Brian's the best,' Aston said and JB agreed too. But Oritsé said, 'No, Stevie Wonder is the best.'

'Well, that's your opinion, for me Brian is better,'

Ten minutes later, as we were on our way to get to our flight we turned the corner to find Stevie Wonder sitting at a table with just one other guy. 'Stevie!' Oritsé exclaimed, hailing him like a long-lost friend.

'All right, man,' said Stevie Wonder, shaking Oritsé's hand. Then he shook hands with us all. Of course, we didn't tell him about the conversation we'd just had, but Oritsé did take his phone number because he said he wanted to work with us in the studio. And then Oritsé lost his phone in LA on that trip and the number went with it, which was a pity.

Oritsé Singing with the Jackson brothers was one of the most incredible moments of my life. It was the closest we came to meeting Michael Jackson and it was amazing to meet the brothers who had such a massive influence on groups like JLS, Boyz II Men, Jodeci and all the other black groups that exist because of them. To perform in honour of Michael Jackson and in his name and to wear his iconic armband alongside his brothers was just mind-blowing. I was just immersed in that performance and I experienced some of the most amazing feelings in my performing career so far.

I remember being there with the boys and thinking, 'This is unbelievable, this is incredible!' We were the only act to perform with the brothers, so it was a real moment and a real honour.

My mum couldn't be there as she was unwell and couldn't travel. So I had a T-shirt printed with the words 'HI MUM' on it and wore it under my stage jacket, just so my mum would know I'd been thinking of her when she saw the concert on DVD.

Marvin Two days after one of the biggest concerts of our career, we went to Uganda on behalf of Sport Relief, which was definitely the most inspiring trip we made. When Sport Relief approached us about making the trip, we jumped at the chance.

It was very real. We saw children dying out there and went to hospitals. It's a weird one because you know you are there for a good reason – you're there to raise money to help stop children dying from diarrhoea – but sometimes you feel it's very intrusive to be in a hospital with cameras when you are seeing parents screaming because their children are either dying or dead. You think, 'Why the hell am I here with a camera crew filming this stuff?' It doesn't seem right to be interviewing people who have just lost their children.

'Am I doing the right thing here? Is this humane to do this?' you think in a moment of doubt.

When that happens, you need to put a different head on your shoulders and remind yourself that you are there to do a job. You are there to bring an experience back to the UK, where that stuff is not normal, to open people's eyes and say, 'This is going on in the world'. The money they can give, whether it's £5 or £20, will stop situations like the ones you are witnessing happening again; it will save hundreds of children's lives. It's important work and we do it because JLS have a voice that is heard and listened to by many people.

The reality over there is that many people live in horrific squalor, in the worst conditions anyone has ever seen or can imagine seeing. We heard stories of children falling in a puddle and dying because the puddles are so contaminated with parasites. Sometimes the only water people can drink is from lakes that have dead carcasses in them – it's just unbelievable.

Oritsé Going to Uganda was very important to me, although I am not directly from Africa: I am half-Trinidadian and half-Jamaican. When I went to Uganda, it was a little reminder of what I'd seen in Nigeria when I went to school there; I experienced a massive heartfelt connection to the people, their problems and situations. I definitely want to go to Africa again and help more. Now the band has ended, there is a lot more that I can do. I admire the humanitarian efforts of people like Bono, Bob Geldof,

Beyoncé, Will.i.am, Stevie Wonder, Prince and Michael Jackson and the way they've used their fame and their talents to help other people.

Marvin It wasn't the safest place in the world. Uganda is a troubled country and I can't say we felt completely safe out there. Every time we entered our hotel, we went through three screening processes. First, they checked underneath the car, then we went through metal detectors and were patted down. We couldn't go out after dark, especially as we were running around with laptops, cameras and phones. Spending time with seriously ill people meant that we also ran the risk of getting ill ourselves, despite being immunised before we went. Still, you can't go there with a protective suit around you and we wouldn't have wanted to.

I remember interviewing a woman who had walked six hours to her local hospital because she had no other way of getting there. Nobody could take her to hospital and her child was very sick with diarrhoea. She was only sixteen and her child was two years old. The baby was really unwell and started developing worrying symptoms because it hadn't been vaccinated when it was born. Just as we were leaving, the baby passed away from a severe case of diarrhoea, which we were told is the biggest killer of young children in Africa. So many people are dying because they are not drinking clean water and they are not immunised.

You have to detach yourself emotionally – it's very hard, especially now I have my own child. Going to Uganda now would probably be more difficult because the only thing I'd think of out there would be Alaia-Mai, who was born in May 2013. But I'm personally quite strong in that way so long as I keep telling myself that the reason I am there is to make a change and to create awareness and help thousands of people.

I think the films we made out there helped to make a record amount of money for Sport Relief. Just knowing we were a part of that was great. If you can help one person you have done a great thing, as we've always said, and we like to think that we have helped more than one person out there. It was an incredible experience for us, and one I probably won't experience again in my life.

Seeing the poverty in this world and how much people are in need changes you forever, especially when you see appeals for donations on TV. Knowing what's out there, seeing what we saw and having first-hand experience, you don't take anything for granted. I will always donate to causes because I know that even £2 or 80p will help towards something. It's great to know that there are those opportunities to help if you can. Even the smallest amount of money can make a difference.

New Horizons

After Marvin proposed to Rochelle Wiseman from The Saturdays – and she said yes! – we went to work on our fourth album, Evolution, collaborating with some of the world's most exciting music producers. Our 4th Dimension tour began in February and by the time it had finished none of us was single anymore! We released the official Sports Relief single of 2012, 'Proud', and performed at the Queen's Diamond Jubilee Concert in June. In July, Marvin married Rochelle and within a few months they were expecting a baby. We released the first single from Evolution and won an incredible fifth MOBO award. It was a life-changing time for all of us.

Marvin Rochelle and I went to the Maldives for the New Year's break in 2011. We chose the Maldives because I'd heard from friends it was the most beautiful place to go. Rochelle had just come off The Saturdays' All Fired Up Tour and we were both very tired – we wanted a really nice, recharge-the-batteries holiday.

I always knew that I was going to propose on holiday. I'd picked the ring in July, almost six months earlier, after many meetings with my diamond man to select the perfect stone, a heart-shaped diamond. I never really knew much about diamonds and there was so much to learn. He showed me so many different grades and cuts, including diamonds that were the same size as one another but some were ten times the price! After I picked the stone I thought was the best, it was made into a ring and stored in a safe. It was tough holding out without saying anything, but I wanted to do things properly. I knew it would be special with Rochelle, but I wanted it to be the best it could be.

We arrived in the Maldives on 28 December and stayed in an incredible hotel for three nights. On New Year's Eve, I hired a small private island in the middle of the clear blue sea. It had one palm tree and was surrounded by the most beautiful crystal-clear waters I've ever seen. Tiny and shaped like an eye, it only stretched about fifty yards by thirty yards, so it was more like a sandbank. The boat from the hotel dropped us off and a couple of the crew set up two daybeds and an umbrella for us. It was almost like lying side by side in the middle of the ocean because there was so little sand and so much sea. It was amazing!

The crew cooked us a great barbecue and off they went, leaving us to relax on our own for three or four hours. I couldn't relax, though – I was just so nervous for the whole day. It's another one of those strange feelings in life that you can't explain, the feeling of nerves before you propose to your girlfriend. Rochelle knew something weird was going on because I wasn't myself, although I don't think she guessed what was coming.

We had the barbecue but I couldn't really eat anything. Luckily, we also had a couple of bottles of champagne, which I *could* drink! After lunch, I led Rochelle to the tip of the island, taking a camera and small tripod with me. I told her that I was setting it up to take a timed photo, but instead I pressed the video record button. 'You've got ten seconds,' I said, running from behind the camera to be by her side. She smiled, expecting the camera to flash, but it didn't. Then all of a sudden I went down on one knee.

I was really nervous now, my heart was thumping. 'I want to make you the happiest man in the world,' I said, stumbling over my words.

'Happiest man in the world?' she said, laughing.

'No, sorry, I want you to make me the happiest woman in the world,' I said. Anyway she knew where I was going. She thought it was really funny that I'd got it all mixed up. Finally I managed to get the most important words out: 'Will you marry me?'

Rochelle started crying. 'I love you,' she said, but she didn't actually say 'yes' to my proposal. I remember it so vividly.

'Is it a yes?' I asked her.

'Of course it is!' she said, jumping on me. I showed her the ring and she loved it. It was a moment of sheer natural ecstasy, really beautiful.

Oritsé In January 2012, we started work on our fourth album, *Evolution*, which is my favourite JLS album. It's the one I play in my car, over and over again. I just feel that on *Evolution* we were able to express ourselves creatively without any kind of barriers or formula. As a result, we got to write and produce and get involved in performing the kind of music we grew up listening to, from old-school R&B to soul, funk and hip-hop. We worked with producers we had never worked with before, like Bangladesh and Rodney Jerkins, so for me it was the record that was most us, the most honest.

When people asked me what we were doing in the studio, I said, 'I'm not going with any formula – I'm just going with whatever comes out of my heart, whatever just comes out of me naturally, music that we love.'

There are a lot of artists who have inspired us, from Michael Jackson and hip-hop influences to Usher and Justin Timberlake, and you can really hear their influences coming through. We wrote some of the album in America and some of it here, the majority of it in Atlanta with Bangladesh.

I felt like finding the single for the last album was the most difficult thing but creating the body of work was the most organic it has ever been for us. A lot of the other times, the single has been easy to find and then the body of work just comes. This time it was a lot more natural. When I hear the *Evolution* album, I hear the JLS when we started out before anybody knew who we were – we went back to our New Jack Swing roots.

Marvin Bangladesh had written massive hip-hop hits for Lil Wayne and Rihanna, so it was amazing to be able to work with him. If you do a search on him and see his discography, it's massive. It was interesting working with him because he was a hip-hop producer who worked 'hip-hop hours'. We come from a world where you start in the studio at midday and you finish anywhere between 6 p.m. and 8 p.m., whereas he started in the studio between 6 p.m. and 8 p.m. and went through to between 6 a.m. and 8 a.m. That was something we had to adapt to because we were entering his world and he has a great reputation.

We tried a different sound on *Evolution* and the results were great. We wanted it to be less pop and a bit more R&B, a bit more back to our original roots, and we really enjoyed making it. It was a great album for us. We are looking forward to taking some of the songs on the road in late 2013 for our Goodbye tour.

In February 2012, we started rehearsing for our 4th Dimension tour. Nobody knows what the fourth dimension is – 4D – and we put together a show that travelled through four different realms: 1D, 2D, 3D and 4D. We wanted a concept that recreated the vibe of a video game and in every realm we collected a winning stone, made of gold or diamond. Every part of the show was different and for the encore we reached infinity, so it was great.

We wanted it to be more than just a concert – we wanted a show with lights and beams and colours, a total extravaganza. Our tours have always been about entertainment, not just concerts where you see us perform our songs. The aim was that when you came to a JLS show, you knew you were going to be entertained and would want to come back again.

When we're touring, we usually have an hour to ourselves before we go on stage. We close the door to our dressing room and then it's just the four of us in our pre-show sanctuary. We listen to music to relax, we do press-ups and body and vocal warm-ups. Often we just have a chat and relax, really. It's a great time for us because everything else is shut away; that hour is about us and the show.

Before we go on, we gather everyone and I say a prayer asking for a great show and thanking God for giving us the energy to do our best. It's something that we have always done, right from the beginning. I come from a fairly religious family and I've always felt close to God and given thanks, spiritually. For us, it's important to continually express gratitude for everything in life and I think it's something we will always do.

Oritsé I lost a dramatic amount of weight before the 4th Dimension tour – what drove me on was knowing people saw me as the chubby one in JLS. I'd always been self-conscious about how I looked – I was constantly covering up or holding my belly in for photos and I wanted to be the best I could possibly be. I also did it for any of my fans that might feel they were overweight, just to prove that you can lose weight if you commit yourself and stay dedicated.

I've got a photo diary on my phone that shows my progression through the diet, which was high on protein and low on fat and carbs. It took a lot of hard work, although I wasn't crazy bad to begin with, just a little bit chubby. It was AJ who helped me transform because she believed in me. I lost so much weight that the boys – everyone – noticed the difference and I felt incredible on the tour because the fans were looking at me as a different person. For the first time ever, I took off my top and showed my abs on stage; suddenly the fans were loving me and were attracted to me – it was as if I was a new member of the band.

When we became friends, AJ said, 'You don't understand yourself.' My style was wrong for me – Ruth used to dress as a rock chick and she moulded me until I ended up looking a bit like a member of Bon Jovi, which I now realise wasn't right for me. AJ changed it up for me and helped swag me out. She had a great vision for me and helped me grow as an artist as well as a person, helping me with my confidence and direction. She'd tell me which clothes suited me and told me to rock New-Era caps but wear them backwards. She has such a good heart – everyone loves her because she is such a good person. She is a *great* person! Some people are jealous of her beauty, personality and talent. They don't really understand how she can have it all, but she has all of those qualities.

AJ's band Vida supported JLS on the 4th Dimension tour. We were still best friends then, but I started to get the feeling that the fans wanted me to be with her. The other boys had girlfriends and I was the only one who was single. The fans were saying, 'Oritsé needs somebody'. They helped push us together by tweeting and messaging. 'Oritsé, AJ loves you. You two should just go out. You two will be cute together,' they wrote. 'I want you two to be together.' 'AJ, I wish you could just go out with Oritsé.' So the fans brought us together and we started seeing each other just after the tour began.

Aston I started dating Sarah, the dancer I'd met a few years before at the Capital Summertime Ball, when she came on tour with us. Every day we were seeing each other, hanging out. We grew closer and closer. Nothing was official at the time, which was fun. Then last summer it started to become more serious.

I liked her and had a huge amount of respect for her, so I thought, 'Why not? I've not had a girlfriend for a long time. Let's try it, let's do it. Let's make it official!' Since then I haven't really looked back, although I just take it a day at a time.

I know I'm not easy to deal with because I like my own space and I like to be with my friends. She recognises that, which is good. We've got a good understanding. I still feel very new to this relationship stuff, but I'm learning. There are times when you have to compromise; there are times when you have to be careful how you phrase things. I've definitely learnt that! It's all good and I've no complaints, but I'm not in any rush for anything like Marvin has right now.

JB The 2012 tour was brilliant. Our tours are about harmony and we've never had any dramas or people kicking off. Often we work with the same dancers and we all go out together in a big group after the show. We have a great time on tour – it's fun and it doesn't seem like work. This time we weren't promoting an album, so there was a lot less promo work to do.

Before you're established, you have to work hard to promote your first singles and albums. You go to all the radio stations around the country, giving interviews. It's just the way it is and you have to get on with it. I need a lot of sleep – I'm one of those people who need eight hours – but needing it and getting it are two different things.

I had to learn to work hard and sacrifice my sleep early... it was part of my growth. We travel a lot; we still appear on breakfast show programmes and do a lot of nitty-gritty promo stuff. I had to learn that lesson and it was part of my growth. There are no regrets as far as I'm concerned – it was all necessary.

The best thing about touring is obviously seeing all the fans. Performing in front of all those people is an unforgettable experience and it makes me smile. I don't revel in the adoration – I guess that's not the way I am – but it's a great feeling to see all those happy faces in the crowd. I don't let it affect my ego; I just feel humbled when I see all those people out there. It's a huge honour to perform for them.

It's a big responsibility when you have a massive effect on people – it's not something you necessarily understand, but it definitely deserves respect from us. It's fantastic meeting our fans and we always spend as much time as we can with them. I will work as hard as I can with the choreography because the fans spend their money and sacrifice a lot in order to get to the concert. This enables us to enjoy the things that we enjoy, so they deserve our best performance in return.

Oritsé During the tour, we took time off to promote our single 'Proud', which was the official Sport Relief single of 2012. 'Proud' for me was directed at everybody who has supported us – family, friends and fans – and about how they feel about us and how we feel about them. For me it's a very powerful song and I think I connect with it the most, partly because of my mum. One night on stage I choked up when I was singing my line and thinking about my mum who wasn't so well at the time. I could hardly sing. Everybody was looking at me and wondering what was going on for me. I had to dig deep in me to sing the rest of my line.

Marvin 'Proud' was a difficult record for us because we recorded and released it during a time of real change at our record label. Nick Raphael and Jo Charrington, the A&Rs who had done such an incredible job managing our first two albums, left Sony to go to London Records and there was a gap before our new boss arrived. So our third album was pretty much A&R-ed by us and our management, which is never a safe place to be in this industry because it can be hard to be objective. You need someone you trust saying, 'That's good, that's rubbish, that's OK'. Nick and Jo had a really good sense of who we were so it hit us hard when they left. I remember when they told us, I thought, 'This is a really big blow.'

They were like management, record company heads, A&R and parents rolled into one. And they were integral to the success and development of JLS, taking us from runners-up on *The X Factor* to award-winning music artists – they played a major part in that. I remember Louis Walsh saying, 'Nick Raphael would be a good person for you to work with.' He founded Another Level and Blue; he's a great guy and he has a great reputation.

I think Nick and Jo's departure still affects us to this day because they were part of the JLS team. Had they stayed at Sony, I think albums three and four would have been different. Don't get me wrong, I love those albums and I really enjoyed making them – I just think things would have been different with Nick and Jo. Still, I can't blame them for leaving. They had their reasons and I understand that. It's just a shame they left when they did.

JB 'Proud' is a stand-alone single, written with the Olympics in mind. Since it was a Sport Relief single, we wanted it to touch as many lives as possible. We wanted it to

be a universal song. I'm very proud of it and it's only slightly behind 'Love You More' in the favourite ballad stakes for me. The 'Proud' video was brilliant and featured Rebecca Adlington, Phillips Idowu and Louis Smith. It was the first video to be filmed in the new Wembley Stadium and we effectively played an empty Wembley, which was fantastic. For me, it was a great video, a great song and obviously a brilliant cause as well. Three in one, I guess!

We toured non-stop for two months solid and then went back to writing and recording the fourth album. *Evolution* was a change, a development. We wanted to do something different. We'd had a turbulent time because we changed labels within Sony, which meant we had new people looking after us musically, a new A&R and everything was new at the label.

It wasn't ideal because we effectively didn't know the people we were putting our trust in and we had a difficult time finding the right first single to make our mark with the album. Eventually we got 'Hottest Girl In The World' but it was a very late delivery of a single. If you look at our first two albums, we had had our first singles at radio in May or June and released them around July, whereas 'Hottest Girl In The World' was looking like an autumn release by the time we selected it.

Marvin Early in 2012, Gary Barlow personally invited us to play at the Diamond Jubilee Concert on 4 June. Gary's a great guy and I think he is a brilliant ambassador for British music – he's heading for the same lane as Tom Jones, Elton John and Cliff Richard. There are not many really talented musicians like him, who can write the best songs, have incredible careers and represent our country fantastically well. I'm 100 per cent sure he will get knighted within the next year or two, especially after what he did for the Diamond Jubilee.

Hundreds of millions of people around the world watched the concert and the only contemporary pop acts on the bill were JLS, Jessie J and Ed Sheeran, so it was a huge honour to be asked. Everybody else was a really big name, from Elton John to Paul McCartney. For us to be on that bill was incredible; we definitely felt lucky to be there.

One of the highlights was when Elton John stopped to chat with us when we passed him. Chris Evans came up with a big Radio 2 microphone and interviewed us right then and Elton was really bigging us up. 'I really like you guys and I want to stay in touch,' he said. That meant so much to us – he is a really nice guy.

After the performance we were invited to go inside Buckingham Palace with two family or friends each. Rochelle was working, so my mum and dad came with me. We were shown into a beautiful stateroom. Everywhere you looked there was a Royal or an A-lister – 'Oh, there's Paul McCartney. Oh, there's Prince William. Oh, there's Sir Tom Jones. Oh, there's the Duchess of Cambridge'. It was so weird how exclusive it was. My mum was blown away by the whole day – she still doesn't stop talking about it. She's a royalist and she loves the royals. She was thrilled to meet Paul McCartney, who was fantastic with her, and I think she had a chat with Prince Edward.

The concert finished at around 9.30 p.m. and we were in the Palace for about two hours. I talked to William and Kate, who said they really enjoyed the show, and I also spoke to Her Majesty the Queen, who said that she hadn't seen us live because we were among the first acts on and she didn't take her seat until the end of the concert. But she said she watched us on the TV screen while she was having her tea, so that was quite cool. It was one of those surreal experiences that you don't want to come to an end, another incredible moment in the life of JLS. Sometimes I forget them and when they come back to me, I think, 'Wow we have experienced some big stuff!'

A month and a half after the concert, Rochelle and I got married at Blenheim Palace in the beautiful, quaint town of Woodstock in Oxfordshire. Like a lot of girls, Rochelle had always wanted to get married in a palace. Years before I came along, she had looked at Blenheim and dreamt about having her wedding there. It's an incredible venue. Set in beautiful surroundings, with gorgeous gardens and a massive driveway, it's a UNESCO World Heritage site and Winston Churchill was born there.

We went for a flying visit the summer before I proposed. It's only forty-five minutes out of London, so very easy to get to. We stayed the night in a townhouse hotel in Woodstock, which was lovely. It only has three bedrooms and the owner wakes up in the morning and cooks you breakfast, which makes it a really homely experience.

We got married on 27 July 2012, about seven months after I proposed. We'd had a really great time planning the wedding. As stressful as it is, it's also a really exciting process.

There was so much to think about, including the catering, music, entertainment, dresses, suits, chief bridesmaids, bridesmaids and ushers. The weather was terrible in the week leading up to the wedding, really bad. On the Wednesday, two days before, it was stormy and raining but then the sun came out on the Thursday. We were really lucky because by Friday the weather was perfect.

It was just the most amazing day, definitely the best day of my life alongside the birth of Alaia-Mai, although I can't really compare them because they are two different feelings. It was just perfect, though.

I felt very emotional when I arrived at the church and made my way up to the altar. It wasn't nerves because I knew it was what I wanted to do – I had no doubts whatsoever. And I can't say I was nervous about being the centre of attention either, because I'm used to people looking at me. What got me choked up was when it hit me that every person in the room was there for Rochelle and me. All of our loved ones and family were there to see us get married and celebrate the unity of two people. That meant so much to both of us.

I was desperate to look at Rochelle as she walked up the aisle – I couldn't wait to see her, especially as we had spent the night before apart and I'd really missed her. She wanted me to turn round and look, but people had told me that it was bad luck, so I didn't see her until she was at my side. She looked breathtaking – her face, her smile, her hair, her dress, everything. It's hard to explain how proud I felt to be about to marry the most beautiful girl in the world. It was the perfect situation – I was so incredibly lucky.

It really was a perfect day. We invited two hundred and fifty people to the wedding breakfast and an additional two hundred and fifty to the evening party, making it five hundred. It was incredible and it all sped by so quickly, though – it was over just like that. I woke up the next day, thinking, 'That was amazing, but where did it go? I want to do it all again.' It's nice that we have a great video of the wedding – we watch it all the time and obviously we'll show it to Alaia-Mai when she grows up.

After the wedding, we only had a week together before Rochelle had to go back to work so we had a mini honeymoon in Portugal, where Rochelle's family own a beautiful villa. I can really understand why people say you need a holiday after your wedding because you spend so much time planning it and getting excited about it then everything comes to a climax on the wedding day and afterwards it all disappears – that's it, it's over. Your body needs time to recharge, so we just relaxed in Portugal for about five days.

Rochelle flew to America to shoot a TV show with the rest of The Saturdays. It was a three-month filming period, so we were going to be apart for ages. I was planning to fly to America and surprise her five weeks into the shoot, but it was still tough to get married and then not see your wife for five weeks. It meant that we didn't really have that honeymoon period that everyone talks about, but we always knew it would be like that – it was one of the sacrifices we had to make to have our wedding when we did and it was worth it.

Rochelle didn't think she was going to see me until she came back to the UK, so it was a total surprise for her when I walked into her hotel room in New York. It was so amazing, especially as Alaia-Mai was conceived there.

After a brilliant week in New York, we came back to the UK and spent a week at home before Rochelle went back to the US. It wasn't long before she started feeling a little bit ill and sensed that something was changing in her body. She came back to the UK because she wanted to see her doctor. We did a pregnancy test at home before we went to the doctor and it was positive. Then we went to the doctor to double confirm and he said, 'Yes, 100 per cent, you are pregnant.' It was just the greatest feeling!

I have friends who have found out that they are expecting a baby and it hasn't been good news – the pregnancy has somehow happened for the wrong reasons and the baby is unwanted. It's never happened to me because I've always been very careful. Now my wife was pregnant and it was something we both wanted. For us, it confirmed that it was in the stars for us to come together. We were both over the moon. It was such a great feeling to be expecting a baby in the right circumstances. We didn't have to panic about how we were going to afford it, or how we would manage. We weren't too crazy busy, which meant we could look after Alaia-Mai and enjoy her. It was all very exciting. There's nothing for us to be stressed out about, other than feeling a bit tired.

We always wanted to do it right – we always wanted to get married first and then have a baby. I have that old-school mentality of doing things the right way. It's what my mum and dad did – they got married and have been together for so long. Rochelle and

I are now on the road to building the same kind of stable, loving family we both want to create.

JB The late release of 'Hottest Girl In The World' in October 2012 was down to lack of a relationship with the new label and the people looking after our project. *Evolution* was a difficult album to make, but I think 'Hottest Girl In The World' was a huge song and deserved to do better than its number six chart position.

We went on to release a double A-side single, but it didn't go to radio in time because we were so up against the deadline and so the tracks didn't have the impact they would normally have had. We were supposed to release 'Give Me Life' but because we weren't happy with how the video turned out, we wanted to release 'Hold Me Down' instead. 'Hold Me Down' is a great single and if it had been released with the right lead times, I'm certain it would have done well. It's my favourite song from the album and people really get behind it when we perform it, partly because it's very aspirational.

Two days before we released *Evolution*, we were back in Liverpool for the 2012 MOBOs, where we won the Best Video Award for 'Do You Feel What I Feel?', our fifth MOBO. It was brilliant! We had such a great night. Despite our problems with the making and release of *Evolution*, it had been another absolutely amazing year for JLS.

A Tough Decision

In late 2012, we reached a turning point. Should we sign with another record label or call it a day for JLS? It was a tough, heartrending decision and we took our time making it. It was hard to accept that JLS was coming to an end, but we've been lucky to have the support of our family, friends and partners to help us come to terms with it. You guys were completely brilliant too. It was so difficult for us all. Ultimately, we want it to be a positive move, so that we can celebrate JLS's achievements and go forward to the next chapter without regrets. There's a lot to be proud of...

Marvin We were the first act from *The X Factor* to see out the duration of their contract. We signed a deal to release four albums and we were about to release our fourth album. Our management said, 'OK, boys, you are out of contract in April, what are you going to do?'

Our lawyer asked, 'Are you going to re-sign with Sony or are you going to look elsewhere?' We were approaching an interesting time in our career.

We knew that if we re-signed, it was going to be another four/five-album deal with a major label and we also knew that Sony had the right to release a greatest hits album, whether or not we supported it. Already we had a tour booked for the end of 2013, which had sold well. It felt like everything was leading to the close of one chapter and the opening of another. The question was: did we want to close the JLS chapter? Opening chapter two would have been a whole new ball game; it would have begun in a time when we didn't have the same hysteria surrounding us. We'd be in a totally different environment with a new label. Our music style would change and we'd be getting older. What did we want to do?

We were told that moving on to chapter two of JLS meant committing for another four or five years. It would inevitably be a hard slog; it would be like starting again if we came back with a new sound and a new image, signed to a new record label. Not everyone was ready for that or wanted to do that. After having so much success, there was a chance that we would be chasing something that would never exceed what we had already achieved.

I can't say that the split happened because of marriage and babies. Rochelle went back to work a couple of months after having Alaia-Mai; The Saturdays are bigger and more popular than they have ever been. JLS could also have continued. It might not have been easy to juggle everything, but Rochelle and I have a lot of support from our families, so we could have managed. So it was more of a career decision than a personal decision. The four of us have always been very different and we're in different lanes now. Everyone had their eyes on different projects and so it made sense to call it a day at the end of 2013.

JB We started discussing our future in November 2012, just after our summer tour ended. We'd had a great year, but now we were at a turning point: what about the next tour and the next label deal? We sat down and started going through all the different options. It wasn't a snap decision because it took us several months to be sure that what we were doing was for the best. It was a very emotional time, but we kept it amicable throughout and I'm sure we came to the right decision.

From the start I have been prepared for the eventuality that we are not going to be together forever. I've looked at this group as my job from day dot and I knew that we probably wouldn't always be relevant. When you look at artists like Sheryl Crow and Bruce Springsteen, although they are still working, they are not relevant in the charts in the same way as they once were. There is a huge difference between what they were doing at their peak and what they are doing now; they still do what they do but their records don't go to number one anymore. I knew there would come a point when JLS would be in that position; I also looked ahead to the time when we would want to get

married and start families, or do individual things and pursue personal passions. I think it would have been foolish of me not to think about that and prepare for it.

Marvin We never wanted to be that band that sticks around and isn't relevant anymore. For a long time we were the biggest thing around but we didn't want to overstay our welcome. We went in on such a high and were so successful that it would have been hard to maintain our success at that level; we had to be realistic. We have never had competition because we are unique, but our peers in our field – other boy bands that are coming through – are undeniably taking a share of the boy-band market.

Many of our fans have grown up. Having said that, I see little girls who are as young as six at JLS concerts and I think, 'You weren't even born when we started!' But the majority of JLS fans were teenagers when we started and are now in their late teens or early twenties so they are discovering new music and new things they like. They have boyfriends and they are not as hormonal as they were – that boy-band hysteria gets lost as the years pass.

We had to be smart about it. If we split up, we could say, 'You know what, we've done incredibly well. We can stick around as JLS and do OK, or we can bow out at the top – heartbreaking as it is – but go out saying we smashed it and achieved nearly everything we wanted to achieve. This way, we can still have a path for our individual careers because we haven't exhausted our JLS career'. It was an extremely tough decision and very sad, but I can hold my hand on my heart and say I think it's the right thing to do. Fast forward five years and I think we will all look back and think it was the right decision.

Oritsé My mum was upset when I told her that JLS were breaking up. 'What about all your fans? They will be devastated! You guys can't break up, it's not fair on the fans,' she said.

'Mum, this is what the situation is now,' I told her. 'Maybe one day in the future we'll get back together, but not right now.' She understood – it's just that she was upset for me and she was upset for the fans. In fact, it's the right time to explore different avenues. We've done a lot together and been together a long time. As Marvin says, 'Don't push it further than it should go.'

We reached a crossroads and a decision was made that we should break up at the end of 2013. Record sales were falling and there was a frustration within the group about the lack of international success. I felt that same frustration, but like anything in my life, I was prepared to fight to overcome it. I'm a fighter – I am always willing to make sacrifices in order to gain something. If that means working twenty hours a day instead of seven, I'm willing to do it.

However, I am in no way negative about the breakup and I think the fact that it has happened means it was meant to happen. I love my boys to bits – they are my brothers. Together, we have been on the most amazing journey; we have done the most incredible things together. We have broken records and we have had success like nobody could have believed. We've sold over ten million records. It's incredible! The most amazing part of it all has been our fans and their love of the band.

Aston We all started out hungry and we got the satisfaction we were looking for. That was incredible, it was well done, and our tours have been amazing. Then, in 2012, I thought, 'Boom, I'm hungry again!' I can't sit and watch the world go by and ask, 'What are we doing today?' I just don't want that right now; I want to be out there as the master of my own destiny, saying, 'Right, I'm doing this and this. I want to conquer this and this'. That's the only way I'm going to get satisfaction now.

I'm here and I love and appreciate what I have, but I'm thinking, 'How do I make this bigger?' Before I joined JLS, I'd think, 'OK, what do I do to get to where I want to be?' Now, again, I'm thinking, 'What do I do to get there?' In a couple of years, no doubt, I will be thinking, 'From here, how do I get to there?' That's just the way I am. I can't help thinking, 'Everything can be bigger, and it can be bigger because I want it to be.'

I haven't got anything to prove to anybody because JLS has been incredibly successful and I love what I do. On the other hand, I can't help thinking, 'Cool, this country has given us the most amazing time ever, but what about the country next to us or the countries on the other side of the world? How would they react to seeing me on stage?'

Once I achieve a goal I've set myself, I think, 'OK, I've done it now.' Then I'll set myself another goal in the week, months or years that follow until I'm thinking, 'God, I need to perform there. I need to do this; I need to write this.' It can be absolutely anything, from a new move to writing the best song in the world, to performing to sold-out stadiums. I'm always moving on to the next target.

I still drive past that first flat in Camberwell where I lived with my two friends. I'm in a totally different car, wearing totally different clothes, but I still have the same mindset. I go out of my way to drive past it. It may seem weird, but I think I need to do it for my own sanity, even though it's in south-east London and I live on the other side of the M25, past north London. I go there to remind myself there was a time when I lived in somebody else's house and only just managed to pay my rent. 'Just remember what you had before and appreciate what you have now,' I tell myself as I drive past.

JB I have still not accepted that we did not make it in America, but for me there is no point in dwelling on the past. It's much better and healthier to work on and develop the things that are happening.

I guess it would have been nice for us to have entered a new record deal and maybe change things up and do things differently so that we could go into a different sphere, another realm. Obviously that was one of the arguments that I brought up with the boys when we decided not to continue what we were doing.

I know what we are capable of. There is no other group in this country – arguably in the world – that can do what we do. I will vouch for that until the day I die. The way we perform, the way we are with each other and the way we are on TV is unique. No one ever watches us and says, 'That was dry, that was boring'. People love watching us on Alan Carr and Jonathan Ross. They love watching us on our own shows, like the JLS documentary and the Christmas show that we did for Sky. I don't want to sound like I'm blowing our trumpets, but I still believe that we can conquer the world, 100 per cent. Whether that will be now or in the future or never, I don't know, but I do know we are capable of it.

Oritsé AJ has been an incredible support to me through the JLS breakup. I'm a great believer that what's meant to be is meant to be. So the breakup is what is meant to be, but that doesn't mean that I haven't been affected by it. Of course I have – I'm the founding member of the band, it's my baby.

AJ and I are living together. We are matched on every level, which is why everybody says she is a female version of me and I'm a male version of her. We're always coming up with new ideas. We DJ together now – we have fun together, we perform together, it's the real thing. She's amazing and I love her. I never thought I'd ever have this with someone.

She is very entrepreneurial. Like me, she is a hustler – she works from the ground up. She's a strong girl and a hard worker. It's been difficult for her sometimes because there have been a lot of obstacles along the way. She used to earn money by working on shows and also teaching – she taught Madonna's daughter Lourdes in performance and also some of the Spice Girls. She's worked at the MOBO Awards, the BRIT Awards and on *The X Factor*. She is incredibly creative and multi-talented, she's been in the studio writing and recording solo material, and she's working on a range for her fashion company, Azari.

Whenever she has doubts, I've been there to show her that she has to continue to believe in herself. She does the same for me when I doubt myself. People don't think that I doubt myself because of who I am, but I do experience uncertainty sometimes. Things have not gone as smoothly as I have wanted them to, at times. As I get older, I don't feel as invincible as I once did.

AJ has taught me to believe in myself. She has spent hours with me in the gym, rehearsing before JLS rehearsals and before tours. I often rehearsed before rehearsals; we became obsessive. Because she's such a good performer, I'd show her what the boys and I were doing for an upcoming video or performance. Sometimes it wouldn't look as good on me as it did on the others and then she'd make it look good on me. She is unbelievable!

I knew that AJ was the one because of the way she was with my mum. When she met my mum, she was very helpful. The turning point came when I had to go away for six weeks with the boys, just at the time my mum needed some care. Mum was staying at my house at the time because the lease on her house had ended. Her health had really deteriorated and I was trying to find somewhere permanent for her to live, where she would be happy and receive the level of care she needed. In the meantime, while I was away, I wanted someone to stay with her 24/7, just to be there and help her out when she needed it.

'I'll stay with your mum while you're away,' AJ offered.

'No, you can't do that,' I said. 'You have your own career and things to do. I will find somebody.'

'No, I'll do it,' she insisted.

Having looked after my mum for many years when I was a kid, I know what a huge responsibility it is to be a carer, especially when it's not even a member of your own family you're looking after. I thought, 'It would be too much of an ordeal for someone like AJ. She is young; she has never had to care for anyone.' On the other hand, I trusted her. I would have trusted her with my life, so I knew my mum would be fine with her.

One day I will definitely have kids with AJ – there is no doubt. She is the only girl in the world that I would trust to look after my future offspring. She means that much to me. There is no one else – I can say that without thinking about it. What AJ and I have is real love.

Everyone talks about the marriage thing, but it's not something I've ever wanted to do. I've always wanted to have kids one day – that has always been part of my dream – but the idea of marriage has never excited me. I'm somebody who acts on my ambitions and the natural progression of things. I don't want to live my life according to conventions or by other people's rules or examples; I want to live in the most natural, progressive way that I can. So if marriage doesn't seem like it's important in that progression, why would I force it? There is no point.

I am the kind of person who will work until they are better and better. I don't want to be the second-best, I want to be *the* best – I have to be the best. I want people to remember Oritsé Williams as somebody who is great at what he does, a master of my art. AJ has always helped me develop and be the best that I can be. She continues to develop me and I help develop her; we help each other and work together to make each other the best that we can be.

I've had to be strong through my mum's illness. I've never complained about it and I've never blamed anything or anyone for it. I've just got on with it and I've tried to do it alone so that it doesn't affect the people around me – my family and friends. I guess that when I go through things, I'm not inclined to share the burden. I feel I can handle it and other people may not be able to handle it in the same way that I can. That's why I tend not to talk to people about my problems.

Now AJ has come into my life and she encourages me to open up – 'Speak to me, let's talk about it'. She shares the burden, which is an incredibly weird feeling. It's great to be able to talk to someone and I think that is what having a partner like AJ means to me. Even when I'm feeling alone, I am never really alone as I know she is willing to share the journey with me.

'Oritsé, if we both lost everything tomorrow, and it was just you and me and we had to live in a cardboard box, I'd be with you,' she says. We call each other Bonnie and Clyde because we will always be together, whatever it takes. Whatever we have to face, we will face it together.

Marvin My wedding was pretty incredible, but seeing Alaia-Mai being born was just amazing! It's the most beautiful experience I've ever had. All the way through the pregnancy, people tell you about the feelings you are going to experience and how amazing it's going to be, but nothing can prepare you for that moment when you first see your child. I went through so many different feelings and emotions; I was on such a high. We are still on cloud nine.

Obviously I knew there was a baby in there when Rochelle was pregnant, but it didn't feel real until I heard Alaia-Mai crying and held her little body in my arms. Wow, that was amazing! A brand-new feeling for me.

Once Alaia-Mai had been delivered, I sat by Rochelle's side while they weighed her and then we held her together. It was just incredible to look at her and think that the two of us had created a real life form.

All we wanted to do was give her kisses and cuddles. It's amazing how quickly you feel love for someone who has only just arrived in your life. I've totally fallen in love with her, to the point where I said to Rochelle, 'For the first time in my life, I'm in love with two women.' And I'm allowed to be, which is nice.

Alaia-Mai was born at 10.05 a.m. on 20 May. She and Rochelle had to stay in hospital for three nights and I was allowed to stay over too, which was great. In most hospitals the man has to go home, but I would have hated to go home to an empty house, leaving my wife and new baby in hospital. A great protective instinct came over me and I couldn't stand the idea of Rochelle being by herself, so it was nice that I could stay and be there for both of them.

A massive feeling of responsibility comes with having a baby and knowing that you will look after her for the rest of your life, or for a good portion of her life until it turns around and she starts to look after us! It's so lovely and we are both so happy and feel so lucky. So far she has been incredible. People keep asking me if I'm having sleepless nights. Obviously I'm tired, but I'm so happy that I don't feel the tiredness. We are very excited and it's all going great.

We are constantly amazed at this little human being that is ours. I expect that feeling will never go away. Every day we see something new in her. We keep looking to see if she looks more like her mum or like me. Apparently, a baby's vision is not great at the start, but about two weeks after she was born, you could see that she was starting to recognise us.

I was on edge when Rochelle and Alaia-Mai took their first day out, to the hairdressers. Every five minutes I kept calling to make sure they were alright, but I suppose I just have to let her go and understand that it's going to happen.

I had a little bit of paternity leave, but little bits and pieces of work popped up which I had to do. It's difficult to tear myself away from Alaia-Mai at the moment because she is so new and Rochelle is still recovering. Like any new parent, I want to be around for every minute of her life but obviously I have to keep working. Still, I guess absence makes the heart grow fonder, if it could grow any fonder. Even if they are asleep it's the best feeling to give them a kiss goodnight.

I would never have entered into a marriage if I wasn't 100 per cent sure that I would stay with my partner. I will stand by Rochelle, as she will stand by me. The honesty, trust, companionship, friendship and the love you share with one another is everything to me and it always will be. It's great for Alaia-Mai that we have that. For me, the worst situation would be to have parents who are not together and it's something that I don't want to happen, so it's important to me to make sure that everything works and we keep our family home beautiful – which it is at the moment – and make it even better.

Aston I went to the hospital when Alaia-Mai was born and I thought she was gorgeous and amazing. Later that night I had to message Marvin: 'In all the times that we've spent together, I've never seen you happier than right now.'

I'd never seen him look so happy as when he was sitting there that first night, holding Alaia-Mai and talking to her while I was talking to Rochelle. I thought, 'I was your wingman when you were trying to get with Rochelle. I know you from before Rochelle, when it was just you and Rochelle and now you, Rochelle and Alaia-Mai.' I think having Alaia-Mai has completed Marvin. He is definitely in a good place.

Marvin Back in 2010, we set up The JLS Foundation to support all of our chosen charities, along with Sport Relief and Brook, among others. We relaunched the Foundation in December 2012 and joined forces with Cancer Research UK, with the aim of raising £2 million over two years to fund research into cancers affecting children, teenagers and young adults. The Foundation will also campaign to raise awareness of cancer in young people and encourage all young people to live active, healthy lifestyles.

On 6 June 2013, we hosted our inaugural OJAM gala ball to raise money for the Foundation. We were nervous in the build-up to it because we had put a lot of time and preparation into it, but obviously our split was announced two months before it took place. Our worry was that we would lose people's interest, or motivation to support us, but we held it together and they stayed on board.

We continued to dedicate our time to organising the event at Battersea Evolution. Soon we had a committee of about twelve people and we had ambitions of Gary Barlow performing on the night and big auction lots – we wanted to raise a considerable amount of money.

When Gary Barlow agreed to perform an exclusive set we were thrilled. We sang 'Back For Good' with him, which was amazing. Dynamo performed, Misha B did a set and I DJ'd at the end of the evening. It was a fantastic event. Our guests included

Keith Lemon, Kelly Brook and David Haye, along with a range of people who have worked with us over the years, from our record company to our management company, to our merchandise company. We wanted people who would really get involved in the night and treat it for what it was: a fundraiser.

We raised over £1 million on the night through auctions and pledges. Nothing could have prepared us for that – it was brilliant! We were very fortunate because there was one extremely wealthy man in the room that night, a guest on somebody's table, who bought two auction lots for £250,000 each. We didn't know him, but he spent half a million pounds on the night. Even if he hadn't been there and we had raised half a million, it would still have been a success but raising over a million pounds broke records. It was Cancer Research UK's biggest night ever for fundraising. It was so good. Without a doubt it was one of the highlights of our career.

A Different Path

We're beginning to come to terms with JLS coming to an end and now we're all looking ahead. What does the future hold? In the short term, we're focusing on our greatest hits album and our last ever tour, which will be our best tour ever and a fantastic JLS celebration with our brilliant, amazing fans. In the long term, who knows? But we've got a few ideas and whatever happens we hope we have the support of you guys. We've still got a lot of fun to have...

Marvin Things could have gone very wrong for us as we approached the band's split. It's a unique situation when you know something is coming to an end. Our relationships could easily have crumbled because we've had to start thinking of ourselves as individuals, which we've never done before. Being selfish changes your approach and the obvious danger is that it will damage your relationships. Luckily, we have too much respect for one another to let that happen. The bond between the four of us is incredibly strong and our sense of brotherhood has meant that we've remained friends and stayed amicable.

We know what is right and what is wrong. That's the way we were brought up and it's the way we lead our lives. So once we knew that JLS were splitting up, there was no chance one of us would have disrespected the band or done something to tarnish the brand. For a start, the other three would have come down on that person like a ton of bricks! None of us wanted that to happen. We are not selfish to that degree; we still respect each other very much. Although everyone has their eye on their own projects now, we want our final tour to be the best tour ever and we're planning to have a fantastic time!

JB We are a group, a working organism. Professionalism and respect are the bottom line. As far as we are concerned, if you have those two things, there is absolutely no reason ever to argue about anything. You can have a discussion and you can disagree with one another. It doesn't need to get to that point where you fall out with somebody – people are different and we have learnt to accept that and respect it.

We have known each other long enough to be able to say what we feel. If one of us is adamant about something, he will reinforce it and keep on reinforcing it. But there comes a moment when there really is no sense in going on hell for leather, trying to prove a point, because it upsets the dynamic. We are a group – everything we do, especially when we are on stage, is about harmony. It really shows if you are not in harmony with each other.

I never see the need to do anything over and above the norm in order to get my point across. You can be passionate about something without crossing boundaries to prove it. For instance, when I played rugby, which is obviously a contact sport, a fight would often erupt when someone stamped on someone else's leg, or pushed him the wrong way. In that situation, I never felt the need to fight. 'You can stamp on my feet as much as you like,' I'd think. 'If I can physically run across the line quicker than you, then I'm going to do it and as a result you are going to feel the humiliation of losing to a nil score.' So instead of getting myself caught up in aggression and negativity on the pitch, I just made sure I didn't lose.

Marvin In early 2013, a series on ITV2 called *The Big Reunion* showed what had happened to groups like Atomic Kitten, Five and Liberty X, who were massive at their peak in the 1990s and early 2000s and are not massive anymore. The programme was interesting on many levels and I think we can use the experiences of people who have had it all and then found that it has disappeared. Some of the interviews painted the music industry to be a really dark, bad place, full of drugs and alcohol. The boys and I haven't experienced that side of the industry. We have never made a secret of the fact that we love having a drink and going out for a party, but we don't do drugs.

Some people become recluses when their success ends. They wander off and sit in a dark room for a couple of years. But I think the four of us are all pretty savvy and switched on enough not to do that. We've created a platform for ourselves in this

country: we are well respected and liked as a group of boys and that's something we can use as a positive to open up different avenues for the next stage of our careers. We've known since early 2013 that JLS are splitting up, which has given us time to set things up for the future.

I have no ambitions to be a music artist anymore. I'm really enjoying my DJing at the moment. I have a weekend show on Capital FM on Friday and Saturday nights and it's going really well; I also DJ at parties and clubs. I was the opening DJ at the 2013 Capital Summertime Ball at Wembley Stadium in front of 80,000 people, which was huge. It was a real buzz to get the party started. I've always liked presenting – I interviewed Michael Bublé and Alicia Keys for *Daybreak*, as well as loads of the artists at the Summertime Ball. I really enjoyed doing it, so I hope it's something I'll do more of.

I'd also like to write and produce, perhaps in a similar way to the dance music producers David Guetta and Calvin Harris. They work by writing an album, bringing in featured artists and producing the whole thing. That's the direction I see my music going, so I'm planning to be creatively involved in a dance record featuring loads of different artists.

Over the years, I've picked myself up in situations where someone else might have crumbled. Having done it before, I know I can do it again, which means that I see this as an opportunity to have a new focus in life. I have a wife and child now and I will pick myself up and go on to the next challenge. It's good that I've never been afraid of hard work, especially as I want to maintain the lifestyle we've become accustomed to.

It's important to have good people around you; family and good friends are vital. Rochelle is great for me – she's in the business too, which means she understands. She is also very good at staying grounded. You have to do normal things and maintain that normality because otherwise you can get wrapped up in a fake world.

It is a double-edged sword because sometimes you have to live up to people's expectations of what it is to be a pop star. There's a certain mystery to it that you maintain by driving flash cars and buying expensive things. You're fulfilling a dream. I remember when I was young and didn't have much, I wanted to buy a nice car and go shopping without worrying about the price of things. But then once you've done it for a year or two, you start to think, 'You know what, this is not the real world and this isn't how things should be.' It's all about balance – there's a fine line between holding onto normality and living the pop star lifestyle. If you can get it right then you have the best of both worlds. I've still got my sports car – that will stick around – but we've also got a couple of 4X4s now.

I feel most grounded when I'm sitting at home with Rochelle and Alaia-Mai, or when we're round at her parents' house or at my parents' house, relaxing with the TV on. I like the feeling of being a normal family, enjoying simple pleasures. You don't feel like a pop star when the baby is screaming at 3 a.m. and you're tired and you have to change a smelly nappy or feed her for half an hour! That's definitely a time I feel very grounded – and very, very happy.

JB I've always been in situations that have been fruitful, thank God. My audition for JLS was my first audition for anything ever and it seems incredible that it led me to where I am now. What happens next? Not knowing is the hardest part of it. Still, I do know that it will be a challenge and I love challenges. What's more, I'm sure I will meet people who will help me along the way, as I have done with the group. We've been lucky to work with some really genuine people – everyone at our management and our label has been great.

I've bought a deer farm in Scotland and I really want to make it self-sufficient, producing all the vegetables and food it needs to maintain itself. It's a new venture and it's very exciting. I can't guarantee whether it is going to work or not, but hope, self-belief and driving determination can get you a long way. We've all had those qualities from the beginning, although we've had moments of doubt, obviously – if we hadn't, we wouldn't be human.

I also plan to build on my property investments, which include two houses in Croydon. Music will remain a big part of my life – I'm still in the studio, still writing and doing what I love to do. I will definitely go on writing, but I'm not going to do anything solo and I'm not going to manage anybody at this stage. I could go a solo route but I don't see the point in doing anything solo because if I'm not going to do something bigger or better than JLS – which, let's be honest, would be a massive feat – it will pale in comparison. People will then talk about the fact that it is paling in comparison, which is something I would never want, because the legacy of JLS is so strong and so beautiful. So I know what I'm not going to do, but I don't know what I am going to do.

Fortunately, there is no rush to do anything. JLS have been very successful, so I have time to consider my options: I can do whatever I want to do.

We didn't announce that JLS were splitting up for our own benefit, we did it for everybody else. We knew what we had decided to do, but we had to explain it to our fans because we've always been open and honest with them. They would have been confused if we had just stopped working together and disappeared without an explanation. They'd be wondering, 'What happened to JLS?' We're very close to our fans and they've given us an incredible amount of support over the years, so it was important to let them know what was happening, and we'll continue to stay in touch via Facebook, Twitter and the JLS Foundation website.

I would say the story is over, although you never know. I think it is, because Marv has started a family and if I do settle down and have a family with Chloe, I don't want to be touring the world. So it either needs to happen soon or for me it's not going to happen. I would perform with the boys again but I can't see myself touring and grafting the way we did in the days when we were doing three gigs a night, especially if I have children. OK, you can travel with kids up to a certain age, if your spouse is with you, but you can't do it beyond a certain point. I love what Take That have done and I love what the Spice Girls have done, but it's just not for me. I don't see myself five years from now saying, 'Yes, let's go back on tour,' because I'll have different priorities then.

Writing a hit song now means following a formula and often you don't have a lot of time in which to do it, so it sometimes feels like there is less creativity in the process than there should be. I would love to have the luxury of taking two or three years to produce an album without having a schedule to follow. On the other hand, it has been good for the four of us to have to write to a timetable – we had the passion and the drive to produce four brilliant albums in a space of five years. It's a great achievement and I'm incredibly proud of all of our songs.

Obviously I will miss the band and everything that comes with it, especially the camaraderie of our working environment. I'm already starting to feel it. It's beginning to hit me that everything is coming to the end and I'm going to be doing things for myself, instead of with my three friends. Obviously we'll still meet up and chill and hang out. Last year I had a Christmas drinks party and all the boys came; I was at the hospital just after Marvin's baby was born. We'll go on meeting at each other's houses and doing summer barbecues. So although we're splitting up, we will still have that family bond holding us together forever. It's like when a child leaves home or a brother or sister goes off to live in another country – people go off to do their own thing, but they are still part of the family, even though they may not be doing everything together, day in, day out, like they once were. In a wider way, that applies to our fans too – we'll always be connected, part of the JLS family.

Aston My mum says there is an extreme amount of luck that surrounds me. No matter how talented she thinks I am – or I think I am – I am a real first-timer. By that I mean anything I go for the first time – touch wood – I usually get. It's amazing how it has happened, all through my life. Now I want to start again. I want to see if it's luck or talent that's powering what I do. It's pretty crazy and I sometimes wonder why I'm doing it but since we decided to end JLS, I've become incredibly hungry again.

I'm tempted to go out there and blitz every single avenue, but I need to hold myself back. Coming from one of the biggest boy bands in the UK, I'm in a strong position and it's in my interests to wait and see who pops up with something to offer. I'd like to do little bits of everything, but it may take time to find out just what I'm capable of. It will give me a knock-back if I'm not offered work straightaway, but then I'll be even more hungry. I know I want to audition again – I keep wondering what it feels like to be in an audition room with people who know that I've sold out the O2 ten times over and done arena tours that have lasted for several months.

Since the band started, I've reached a new level of confidence. My ambitions don't just extend to America, they're international; I'm looking at Asia, Europe and Africa too. Anywhere, everywhere! I love this country to bits, but as an artist there are only so many times you can play at the O2 Arena and still have that first-time feeling. I count our blessings every day and I'm so appreciative of everything we've done, but I'd like to play the Sydney Opera House and Madison Square Garden as well.

I'm more than hungry for that international success and I believe it's very much within my grasp, even though I'm back to square one. I want to do what I'm already doing, but on a far bigger scale. When I turned twenty-five, I looked around the industry and thought, 'There is nobody my age who does what I want to do.' Everybody is a little bit older than I am. They are the opposite of how I look, how I act and how I am, which makes me think I've got to go for it.

When I look at some of my idols, it's clear they were never satisfied. They kept wanting to get better and better. I really admire Will Smith's career path. First he was in a TV sitcom, next he was a rapper and then he made the transition to film. Once he was in film, he accepted certain roles so that he could move into a position where he could choose the roles he actually wants, which led to producing and directing. He can do whatever he wants now, but no matter what role he plays, he will always have that Fresh Prince stamp because it's where he started as an actor. Everyone loves that about him.

I don't know if I have grown up a massive amount as a person in the last five years, but I think I've grown up professionally. I love what I do and I love being part of this world and this industry; I couldn't do anything else. Years ago, when we first started, I might have said, 'I'd still love to play football.' Now I think, 'This industry is definitely right for me – professionally, socially, mentally and physically.' My mentality is right for this industry, more so now than it was five years ago.

It's great because everybody loves JLS and I'll be happy to be the little young one in JLS forever. I will never turn around and say that I'm not in JLS. Even ten years from now, I'll be saying, 'Yes, I am: I'm in JLS. But this is also what I can do.'

Our final arena tour is going to be happy but very, very emotional. It's going to be so hard to say goodbye to our wonderful fans, but we also hope that it will be a huge celebration of what we've achieved with their amazing support. It says a lot that we're saying goodbye on an arena stage and it's all thanks to the JLSters – we love them all so much.

Oritsé Everybody asks me the same question: 'What are you going to do next?' It seems to be the question on everybody's lips and I can't really answer it right now. People say they know what the other three are doing, but what is Oritsé going to do? They say Oritsé could go down so many different avenues. 'Are you going to do music? Are you going to do management?'

What I will say is that I came into music with a passion. Ever since I was a child, I wanted to earn money by being creative and making music. I had no experience of the music business but I was determined to make it in music, singing and songwriting. So

I came into the industry with love, ambition and determination. Now I want to remain in the business and I want to build my company; I want to be in it for the long term. I'm not thinking about the short-term goal, but the long-term goal. I want longevity in my career and I believe I can make it happen.

For months I've been training for two hours a day. I'm doing everything, even yoga, to keep the weight off and for a sense of general wellbeing. I put on weight fast because my metabolism is slow, so it's a constant fight with me. Some people fight it, some people don't. I believe that you can kickstart your metabolism into a higher gear with exercise and by eating regularly.

I love all of JLS's fans. I read their letters and I keep their fan mail. I've got stacks of fan mail at home. If I don't have a chance to read it when it arrives, I save it until I find a day to read it because someone has put time and effort into writing me a letter and putting their heart and soul on paper, and it's somebody who looks up to me. I would never throw fan mail in the bin. No way! That's not me.

At the time of writing, we still don't know what our final single will be or even if we are going to have a next single. If we are, it has to be memorable because it's the last single people will remember us by. Our final tour is going to be emotional and nostalgic; it's going to be a celebration of everything we have achieved over the last six to seven years. It's going to be a collection of memories and special moments and it's going to be the tour where we just have fun! There is nothing boring about what's coming next – we are going to have fun and enjoy every minute up until the end!

Marvin We are signing off and we have to sign off with a banger, something that's going to seal our legacy. It's got to be our best song ever, so we are feeling the pressure. You know what you are going to get with the album because it's the *JLS Greatest Hits* album, but still we need enough excitement around it for people to say, 'You know what? I need to buy this last piece of JLS.' So the final single is a very important single for us. We want people to be saying, 'Have you heard the new JLS record? It's amazing!' We want them to feel the same way about it as they felt when they first heard 'Beat Again', 'Everybody In Love', 'She Makes Me Wanna' or 'Hottest Girl In The World'.

I look at my awards cabinet at home and I think, 'Wow, we have done so well!' It is really amazing and hard to believe that we have two BRITs and five MOBOs. The JLS stats are incredible. Five albums, 10 million units and seven top awards – we have our fans to thank for it all! If it wasn't for them, someone else would have their names go down in music history instead of us. Because of our fans, we will never be forgotten – and we'll never forget that we owe all our success to them.

For us, the JLS Foundation is probably the most important part of the JLS legacy. The band may be coming to an end in 2013 but the Foundation will carry on and we will come together annually as a four-piece to support it and continue to raise money and awareness for different causes. We've all agreed to it.

Our Goodbye tour will be a huge, positive celebration of everything we have achieved and experienced as a band. We have had seven incredible years. We've gone through so much together and witnessed some incredible things, so there's a lot to celebrate. We'll be thinking, 'We did good, boys – we smashed it! Let's go out there and put on the best show possible for our fans and go out on a high.'

The last show of the tour is at the O2 Arena, where we first auditioned for *The X Factor*. We've come full circle. How poignant it is that we're finishing our career at the very place we started it.

JB We're sad to say goodbye, but there's so much to be proud of. We've gone from singing at family parties to selling out 40-date arena tours. And we managed to transcend *The X Factor* and grow and develop into a multi-million selling act. We did it because we believed in ourselves, supported one another and had the full backing of our families. But the people we want to thank most of all for our success are our amazing, incredible fans because we couldn't have done any of it without them. You're the people who made everything possible for us, so we wanted to end the book with a special message to you all...

★ ★ ★ ★

Goodbye, With Love

Right from the beginning we've known that JLS fans are very, very special, the best fans a band could ever have. You have always been there for us. It's unbelievable how loyal you've been. You voted us through week after week on *The X Factor* when we were just starting out and then you came to see us in clubs up and down the country before we had a record deal. It's because of you that our first single, 'Beat Again', went straight to number one, followed by our second single, 'Everybody In Love' and our debut album, *JLS*. It still seems hard to believe everything that's happened over the last six years!

It's because of you that we've sold ten million records, had five number one singles and won two BRITs and five MOBOs, not to mention our bestselling DVDs and books. It's also down to you that we were crowned Britain's hardest-working band two years running, because we wanted to perform live to as many of you as we could. You light up our shows with your energy and love. Life doesn't get any better than when we're on stage performing for you.

Thank you for all your support and love over the years. We feel so lucky and we're so grateful to you for buying our records and coming to our shows. It's been the most incredible journey and your letters and messages have kept us going every step of the way. We will never forget that all our achievements have been made possible by you.

We hope you've enjoyed the book. The title is taken from one of our favourite JLS singles, 'Everybody In Love', the song that we feel best describes our feelings for our fans. We still get goosebumps when we perform it. That's because, no matter what, we will love you all forever – in fact longer than forever! Never forget that. We wish you every happiness in your lives and we hope you fulfill all your dreams and ambitions, just as you've made many of our dreams and ambitions come true. You believed in us and we believe in you and we'll always be there for you in one way or another, just as you've always been there for us.

It breaks our hearts to be writing this, but we hope you understand that this is the best thing for JLS and for each of us individually. We wanted to go out on a high and do our fans proud in every way, as we've always tried to do, right from the start. It's so hard to say goodbye, especially as all we really want to say is a huge thank you from the bottom of our hearts, for everything. You've been the most amazing fans in the world. We love you all!

Discography & Awards

Studio Albums

Title: **JLS**
Release date: **9 November 2009**
Label: **Epic**
Chart position: **1**

....

Title: **Outta This World**
Release date: **22 November 2010**
Label: **Epic**
Chart position: **2**

....

Title: **Jukebox**
Release date: **14 November 2011**
Label: **Epic**
Chart position: **2**

....

Title: **Evolution**
Release date: **5 November 2012**
Label: **RCA**
Chart position: **3**

....

Compilation Albums

Title: **Goodbye: Greatest Hits**
Release date: **18 November 2013**
Label: **RCA**

Singles

Title: **Beat Again**
Release date: **2009**
Album: **JLS**
Label: **Epic**
Chart position: **1**

....

Title: **Everybody in Love**
Release date: **2009**
Album: **JLS**
Label: **Epic**
Chart position: **1**

....

Title: **One Shot**
Release date: **2010**
Album: **JLS**
Label: **Epic**
Chart position: **6**

....

Singles

Title: **The Club is Alive**
Release date: **2010**
Album: **Outta This World**
Label: **Epic**
Chart position: **1**

....

Title: **Love You More**
Release date: **2010**
Album: **Outta This World**
Label: **Epic**
Chart position: **1**

....

Title: **Eyes Wide Shut**
(featuring Tinie Tempah)
Release date: **2011**
Album: **Outta This World**
Label: **Epic**
Chart position: **8**

....

Title: **She Makes Me Wanna**
(featuring Dev)
Release date: **2011**
Album: **Jukebox**
Label: **Epic**
Chart position: **1**

....

Title: **Take a Chance on Me**
Release date: **2011**
Album: **Jukebox**
Label: **Epic**
Chart position: **2**

....

Title: **Do You Feel What I Feel?**
Release date: **2012**
Album: **Jukebox**
Label: **Epic**
Chart position: **16**

....

Title: **Proud**
Release date: **2012**
Album: **N/A**
Label: **Epic**
Chart position: **6**

....

Title: **Hottest Girl in the World**
Release date: **2012**
Album: **Evolution**
Label: **RCA**
Chart position: **6**

....

Awards Won

⭐ **2007 Urban Music Awards**
Best Unsigned Band

⭐ **2009 MOBO**
Best UK Newcomer / Best Song, *Beat Again*

⭐ **2009 BBC Switch Live Awards**
Switch's Outstanding Artist

⭐ **2010 BT Digital Music Awards**
British Group / Best Video, *Everybody In Love*

⭐ **2010 BRIT Awards**
British Breakthrough / British Single, *Beat Again*

Awards Won

⭐ **2010 MOBO Awards**
British UK Act / Best Album

⭐ **2010 Urban Music Awards**
Best R&B Act / Best Group

⭐ **2011 BT Digital Music Awards**
Best Video, *Eyes Wide Shut*

⭐ **2012 MOBO Awards**
Best Video, *Do You Feel What I Feel?*

When we decided to write our very last book, we knew one thing we definitely wanted to be in there – you guys! Our fans have been the best a boy band could ask for and supported us through everything. We asked you all to write to us with your own JLS memories and what JLS has meant to you. It's been really emotional reading through all of your letters. It's reminded us of just how many special moments we've shared together. We'd love to print each and every one but that would be one massive book! So we had to pick one of our favourites. Meet Eden Henderson-Roe, 15, from Tolleshunt Major, Essex; she is a true JLSter who embraces the love and spirit of our band and all of our fans. Thank you Eden for always being there!

I've been the ultimate JLS fan since 2008. I remember watching four talented guys on X Factor and instantly loving them. I'm so proud knowing that I've been part of this huge JLS family that has evolved immensely from the beginning until the very end. During this time I've tried to support you as much as I can and have driven everyone I know insane with my crazy, admittedly obsessional, love for you. It's been my dream to meet you for a long time and I'll not give up. You've been such a massive inspiration to me over the last five years and a huge part of my life. I'm absolutely devastated knowing JLS will be no more. I'm so proud of what you've achieved, as a group and individually, and will look forward to seeing your success in the future. Having M.E. for ten years and relying on a wheelchair outside of my house has been hard and I often feel down, but listening to your music and watching your funny interviews never fails to make me smile. Thank you especially to Oritsé for giving me strength. I empathise with your personal struggles and you inspire me to continue to be positive. I've so many happy memories of you as you mean so much to me. Thank you to you all for being my inspirations and I'll continue to follow each of your journeys. I wish you all the best of luck Aston, Marvin, JB and Oritsé for your exciting futures ahead. Victory after victory, triumph after triumph!

We would also like to say a special thanks to all of these JLSters who have given us so much of their time, love and support too. We know there are a lot more of you out there as well, so if your name isn't here but you're reading this then thank you to you too!

Aasta Williams, Abbey Wilkinson, Abbie Daniel, Abbie G, Abbie Young, Abbie-Rose Motion, Abby Ann Watt, Abi Hodgettes, Abie Baxter, Abigail Shilcock, Abiha Khan, Aimee Blackburn, Aimee McCallum, Aimee Moore, Aisha Ali, Alana McKenna, Aleena Mahmood, Alex Dickinson, Alex Kelly, Alex Lane, Alex Wake, Alice Cooke, Amber McEwan, Amber Moore, Ammi Karia, Amy Burdett, Amy Graham, Amy Rowe, Amy Selvey, Andrea Howard, Angel Nicholson, Anjni Vekaria, Annabel Dodd, Annalise Jee, Annalise Warnock, April Wilson, Arianne NG, Ashe Murphy, Ashleigh Morritt, Ashleigh Spillane, Becky Sheead, Becky Spencer, Belinda Webb, Bethan Jones, Bethany Ashman, Bethany Train, Bethany Welsh, Cait Ramsay, Caitlin Blackwell, Caitlin Stiles, Caoimhe Clinton, Cara Lock, Carly Louise Lloyd, Casey Rodway, Catherine Marshall, Celine Williams, Chanel Elven, Channelle Carmichael, Chantelle Morris, Charlie Cook, Charlie Potts, Charlotte Gibson, Charlotte Hallam, Charlotte Pullen, Charlotte Walton, Chelsea Louise Mullan, Chelsea Ryan, Chelsea Walker, Chloe Addison, Chloe Bird, Chloe Ellis, Chloe Fisher, Chloe Fletcher, Chloe Foster, Chloe James, Chloe Lamey, Chloe Lay, Chloe Longworth, Chloe McGachan, Chloe Mcmeekin, Chloe Mirfin, Chloe Price, Chloe Wallis, Christie Cohen, Christina Powell, Christina Searson, Chyna Wills, Ciara McNamee, Clair Jones, Connie Murray, Coral Lopez, Courtney Smith, Danielle Davies, Danielle Macleman, Danni Foskett, Demi Leonard, Demi Welsh, Devon Coles, Eden Henderson-Roe, Eleanor Ward, Eleanor M.Cooper, Elise Butcher, Elita Gashi, Ella Claire Surman, Ella Hudson, Ella Jane Panting, Elle Carcavella, Elley Renton, Ellie Lambourne, Ellie McKenzie, Elysia Knight-Francis, Emilie Palmer, Emily Locke, Emily Rhodes, Emily Richardson, Emily Robins, Emily Shearstone, Emily Whittaker, Emily Wright, Emma Baker, Emma Claire Lister, Emma Hollamby, Emma Jackson, Emma Weir, Emma Wilson, Emma-Jane Paton, Erica Ward, Faaizah Patel, Faaizah Ukaye, Fauzia Saddiq, Fiona Hepworth, Freya Robey, Gemma Dignam, Gemma Hume, Gemma Louise Dale, Gemma Reid, Gemma Tollerfield, Georgia Goodley, Georgia Knott, Georgia Murgatroyd, Georgia Musty, Georgia Ormond, Georgia Williams, Georgina Bowden, Georgina Hughes, Gillian Wilson, Giorgia Sullivan, Grace Hanlon, Grace Morris, Greer Downey, Hannah Dunphy, Hannah Parker, Hannah Porter, Hannah Reynolds, Hannah Rumble, Hannah Stanyer, Hannah Wrigley, Harriet Bowers, Harriet Messenger, Hayley Cinnamond, Heather Train, Hollie Laker, Hollie Woodford, Holly Goddard, Holly Holmes, Holly Wheeler, India Hinsley, Isabelle Westlake, Jade Bickerton, Jade Stenton, Jade Upshall, Jasmine Sutton, Jaymi Lacey, Jayne Sanders, Jemma Key, Jemma Parsons, Jenna Duffy, Jennifer Henry, Jessica Brookes, Jessica Louise Haines, Jessica Rose Lyons, Jessica Rose McGuirk, Jessica Smith, Jessica Waters, Jodie Hearne, Jordane McVeigh,

Karen Dardis, Kasha, Kate Williams, Katelyn Gent, Katie Bevan, Katie Sandiford, Katrina Bamber, Katy Timson-Sheppard, Kayla Somerville, Kayleigh Gibson, Kelly Jay Merchant, Kelly-Anne Roscoe, Kelsey Russon, Kiera Louise, Kiera Thyra, Kimberley Roberts, Kira Payne, Kiran Gill, Kirsten Coleman, Kirsten Lyall, Kirsty Dickinson, Kirsty Fox, Kirsty Guest, Krista Sim, Krupa Patel, Kylie Garden, Kyra Ikins, Laila Kurn, Laura Anna Wain, Laura Carden, Laura McCauley, Laura Thompson, Lauren Ashworth, Lauren Cooper, Lauren Iles, Lauren Roxburgh, Lauren Thirsk, Lauren Wright, Lauren-Jade Frost, Leah Mcallister, Leah Slater, Leeanne Hambleton, Leia Branch, Leonie Wong, Libby Standbridge, Lila Tamea, Lisa Li, Lisa Quick, Lizzy Rakestraw, Louisa Warnham, Louise Weeks, Lucie Cripps, Lucky Nisha Uddin, Lucy Albon, Lucy Collins, Lucy Kew, Lucy Mckeegan, Lucy Mcnulty, Lucy Robbins, Lucy Robinson, Lucy Sawyer, Luisa Amasanti, Lydia Matulka, Lydia Waddleton, Maddie Dillon, Maisie Ward, Maria Henderson, Marie Charnley, Maryam Khan, Meera Chouhan, Megan Cook, Megan Beale, Megan Brewster, Megan Devereaux, Megan Gardner, Megan Hardy, Megan Louise Dawson, Megan McDonald, Megan Owens, Megan Venturi, Melissa Bell, Mezubin Kadar, Micheala Crocker, Michelle Grant, Millie Wright, Mimi Ahmed, Mollie Catlin, Mollie Maddox, Molly Grace Webster, Molly Jean Larkin, Molly O'Shea, Montana Pusey, Morgan Robbins, Naomi Johnston, Naomi Sheppard, Natalia Thomas, Natalie Crane, Natalie Dickens, Natalie Pounder, Natalie Wong, Natasha Rudd, Natasha-Marie Moore, Nerissa Vaughan, Niamh Gough, Niamh McCrory, Nichola Gilmore, Nicole Berman, Nicole Hendry, Nicole Page, Nicole Ormond, Olivia Baldwin, Olivia Hayward, Olivia Murrain, Olivia Partridge, Olivia Rose Busby, Olivia Shaw, Olivia Smith, Olivia Thorpe, Olivia Watson, Paige Barrett, Pippa Mulldon, Polly Nunn, Poppy Murphy, Prabhjeet Gharyal, Rachel Dempster, Rachel Press, Rachel Sanders, Rachel Smith, Rebecca Booth, Rebecca Cox, Rebecca Dyer, Rebecca Horton, Rebecca Sweetman, Rebecca Wright, Rebekah Fraser, Rebekah Saynor, Rhiannon Fancett, Rhianon McCann, Robyn Makin, Rochelle Cross, Roisin Henderson, Roohie Humes, Roop Kalkat, Roopa Vyas, Rubina Begum, Samantha Jane White, Sarah Coleman, Sarah Darby, Sarah Harwood, Sarah MacInnes, Sarah Moore, Sasha White, Savanna Leigh, Scarlett Daniels, Scarlett Sharp, Sehrish, Seren Dakota Roberts, Serena-Lianne McGill, Shani Bennett, Shanice Gilmore, Shannon Bayliss, Shannon Higgott, Shannon Pallan, Shannon Tyne Elliott, Sharan Virdee, Sharlene Campbell, Shaunna Carney, Simran Mann, Skye Scobie, Sneha Mervana, Sonia Popat, Sophie Gray, Sophie Hannah McCutcheon, Sophie Hutson, Sophie Scott, Sophie Hey, Stacey Gandy, Stacey Lea Hibbins, Stacey Ross, Steph Buckley, Stephanie Kirman, Subeyda Abdalla, Sumaiya Kassam, Sydnee Brook Power, Tamanna Islam, Tamsin Barnes, Tamzin-Leigh Hoath, Tara Brazier, Tasha Croad, Tashinga Muzuva, Teri Gowan, Theresa Joce, Tiffany Elliott, Tiffany Horth, Tori Ruddle, Vicky Liney, Victoria Bell, Victoria Louise Morel, Vikki Blackburn, Xander May...and every other JLSter there has ever been.

Picture Credits

★ Opening Pages

★ Boy Dreamers

★ Magic in the Room

★ One Last Chance

★ Whirlwind

★ *Top of the World*

★ *In Different Worlds*

★ *Far and Wide*

★ *New Horizons*

Picture Credits

★ *A Tough Decision*

★ *A Different Path*

Modest!

JLS are exclusively managed by Richard Griffiths, Harry Magee
and Phil McCaughan for Modest! Management